Managing Today's Public Library

Managing Today's Public Library
Blueprint for Change

Darlene E. Weingand

1994
LIBRARIES UNLIMITED, INC.
Englewood, Colorado

Office
025. 1974
W423m

Copyright © 1994 Darlene E. Weingand
All Rights Reserved
Printed in the United States of America

No part of this publication may be reproduced, stored in
a retrieval system, or transmitted, in any form or by any
means, electronic, mechanical, photocopying, recording,
or otherwise, without the prior written permission of the
publisher.

LIBRARIES UNLIMITED, INC.
P.O. Box 6633
Englewood, CO 80155-6633
1-800-237-6124

Library of Congress Cataloging-in-Publication Data

Weingand, Darlene E.
    Managing today's public library : blueprint for change / Darlene
E. Weingand.
    x, 185 p. 17x25 cm.
    Includes bibliographical references (p. 173) and index.
    ISBN 0-87287-807-4
    1. Public libraries--United States--Administration. I. Title.
Z678.W45   1994
025.1'97473--dc20   94-4454
                                                              CIP

Contents

APR 1 3 1995

36.00

Preface

My earlier book, *The Organic Public Library,* was conceived in response to a need—specifically, my personal search for a text I could use for my class, The Public Library. In an effort to portray the public library as a "mosaic of functions, opportunities, contributions, and resources that must be seen in its complex wholeness," I divided the text into two main sections: "Foundations" and "Putting into Practice," with parallel chapter construction.

I still believe in the underlying premises of that first work, but the intervening years have clearly demonstrated the critical need for sound management principles in the administration of public libraries as citizens and governmental units require increasing levels of accountability. Although these management principles do need to be grounded in the breadth of real-life practice, the public library's entrance into a new decade heralds the need for a new look at what public libraries are all about and how they can most effectively become central to the communities they serve.

Therefore, in this text I extract concepts and relevant passages from *Organic,* but I then meld these elements into a unified approach to public library management that is grounded in a marketing response to community needs. There is sufficient change and new material so that this book cannot be termed a "second edition." In *Organic,* I described the public library as a "complex institution, evolving through many decades of human history and colliding today with the perplexing realities of change, declining funding, and shifting purpose." The complex nature of public library service will continue to be a fundamental consideration, but here it is treated as an opportunity for excellence and diversity rather than as a series of problem areas. Further, those "perplexing realities" have the potential for fostering growth and maturity of organizational purpose and are discussed in that light.

There are 10 chapters, each addressing a different aspect of public library management. Although the chapters have the foundation of basic management theory, they are written with particular emphasis on public library operations. The focus throughout is on the library's client and on using planning and marketing strategies to assess and meet identified community needs. Technologies, though ever-present, are considered in terms of effective library management.

The reader who is familiar with *Organic* will note the continuance of "Scenarios"; in addition, "For Discussion" questions are included. Further, I encourage the reader to give thought to the longer case studies that have appeared in the library press, such as the fictional *River Bend in Transition: Managing Change in Public Libraries.*[1]

Whereas *The Organic Public Library* was conceived of primarily as a textbook for library school students, this completely revised work is designed to serve as a primary source for public library personnel at all levels of management, in libraries serving communities of varying sizes. The importance of using sound management principles in the administration of public libraries has grown in concert with a rapidly changing society. However, even as the theories and practices of management continue to evolve, the basic tenets remain constant; it is the application of those tenets that creates the environment of the organization and the interactive bridges between the library and its community.

The public library in the United States has a proud heritage. It now stands upon the threshold of unparalleled opportunity as the much touted Information Age takes hold of society. I hope this book will help library managers identify existing strengths and build upon them to more clearly and dynamically serve their clients. The potential is excellence; the potential is positioning the public library as an essential service in every community; the potential is reachable—through creativity, effort, and vision.

NOTES

1. Bruce A. Shuman, *River Bend in Transition: Managing Change in Public Libraries* (Phoenix: Oryx Press, 1987).

# Evolution of
a Mission

Alvin Toffler has dubbed today's world the "Third Wave," a wave of information that overrides and subsumes earlier waves of agriculture and industry.[1] The rise of this information age is as profound a cultural development as were the agricultural and industrial economies that preceded it. Public libraries can be in the forefront of this new age, for the organization and dissemination of information and knowledge are their natural functions.

Moreover, the public library has a special role to play in the information age, a role that must be grounded in the social and political environment of the community it serves. Many forces—both internal and external to library operations—are in play, and no public library can operate in isolation from them. But the effective library manager will respond by melding the public library's unique capability and potential with the emerging needs, technologies, and values of the community. Client needs and interests will be the energy that fuels library resources and actions.

Because no two communities are exactly alike, the Public Library Association, a division of the American Library Association, has redirected its attention from a focus on standards to an emphasis on the planning process as a strategy for effective interaction with the community.[2] It is within such a planning process that good management—which has been variously described as a science or as a set of skills—can be most productively accomplished. The context of a planning process also makes room for the art of management: the capacity for interweaving techniques, vision, and the subtleties of human communication.

The initial step in planning is the formulation of the mission statement. Although this sounds straightforward, the discussion that precedes the actual writing of the statement may well be the most time-consuming portion of the entire process.

THE QUESTIONS

At first glance, the mission statement responds to the question "Why?" Why exist? Why serve? Why behave in any certain manner? Yet closer scrutiny reveals other questions as well—questions that provide the basic information regarding any situation or event.

- *Who* shall be served?
- *Where* shall service be located?
- *When* shall service be available?
- *What* services/products shall be offered?
- *How* shall access be provided?

These additional questions are addressed further along in the process, but awareness of their existence is essential in the deliberations attending the question "Why?" None of these supplementary questions can be answered adequately before the "why" is addressed; indeed, they are fairly irrelevant unless the institutional purpose has been articulated.

A look backward can add a depth of understanding of today's public library. History and tradition are benchmarks on a continuum of time—a continuum that flows from our earliest libraries through the vagaries of a changing society.

YESTERDAY'S PUBLIC LIBRARIES

From the subscription libraries of the 1700s to the nineteenth-century community and mechanics' apprentices libraries and the pioneering Boston Public Library of the 1850s, the public library in America has grown into a flexible institution—reflective of the times and chameleonlike in its response to social persuasion.

Early public libraries were situated primarily in urban settings and supported in large part by philanthropy. By the Civil War years, the free public library was as established a part of the American cultural and educational system as the once-controversial idea of tax-supported universal public education.[3] In addition, the rising democratic sentiment of the late 1800s demanded free access to books for the entire population.

As the original purpose of public library service, education, was joined by two other aims—recreation and information—in the late nineteenth century, confusion arose as to which objective was paramount. This lack of conviction resulted in citizen perception of the public library as a junior partner in educational endeavors at a time when inadequacies in the urban environment were encouraging recreational reading as a "socially useful" activity.[4]

The early twentieth century saw an increase in the social consciousness of the library. Personal reader's guidance was provided to World War I servicemen, and foreign language books, programs of citizenship and Americanization, and books in English for new readers were made available in response to the influx of immigrants.[5] Andrew Carnegie's generosity in erecting public library buildings was also well timed in extending library services to a larger percentage of the total population.

In the next three decades, the multiple dislocations of prosperity, depression, and war—and accompanying technological developments and social change—created a crisis-prone nation, convulsed with disorder and insecurity. These pressures prompted public library response in areas of personal development, vocational improvement, and civic affairs. However, the library's perception of its audience varied from a vision of a community of knowledge seekers (a "people's university") to an American Library Association-defined "small but select group of natural library users."[6] The mission of the public library remained confused.

In the 1950s and 1960s, federal dollars were a stimulus to library construction and outreach. The public library began to extend services to the previously unserved: minorities, the disabled, the aged, the illiterate, the institutionalized, and the economically deprived.[7] The 1970s and 1980s were far less kind, and economic retrenchment became the unhappy rule for many public libraries. Few engaged in formal planning activities; reactive response to crisis seemed to be standard managerial practice.

Every organization operates according to a mission. This mission may exist in the mind of one or more persons or actually be written on paper; either way, this subjective sense of "why" is universally in place. The fundamental weakness of most organizational perceptions of purpose lies in omission, rather than commission. When such organizational philosophy is constructed internally, without adequate research of the external environment, the result can be internal harmony and external dissonance. Consequently, when a library prepares to enter into a planning process, the staff must be alerted to the very real possibility that the library's perceived mission may be modified.

In fact, all players in the planning exercise should be operating under the assumption that every phase is written in sand, not stone, and thereby subject to continual revision.

However, planning is a recent footnote in library history. What has caused the public library to even consider rethinking its position in U.S. society and culture?

THE EMERGENCE OF A
PLANNING MINDSET

Despite an evolving sense of social responsibility by librarians, confusion as to the public library's mission has persisted. Less than one-third of the nation's population can be numbered among public library clients, and frequently the percentage is much lower. This less-than-desirable condition is often the result of confusion and ignorance related to the library's perceived mission, both internally and externally. Efforts at planning and developing answers to the "why" question are just beginning to emerge.

It is only in the second half of this century that planning at any level in libraries has become formalized, with the initial impetus coming from general management in the private sector. There are several reasons for this acknowledgment of the importance of planning. First, private companies have found that systematic examination of a complex and changing environment has produced positive results. The combined knowledge and talents of many people have served to more readily identify those variables of opportunity and threat that are the natural by-products of rapid change. Second, planning has forced managers to ask the right kind of questions, such as "What is our line of business?" and "What are our objectives?" Finally, planning has been seen as a logical way to create the future on paper—if what is written is not acceptable, one can erase it and start again.[8]

The discovery of formalized planning by the corporate sector has affected other arenas of management, including nonprofit agencies. Because of the benefits perceived by business, formalized planning is now becoming part of the managerial consciousness of a variety of organizations, including libraries. This is particularly true in the 1990s, when the concept of excellence is receiving so much public attention.[9]

Planning can be viewed as a road map. Engaging in a systematic planning process eliminates a random or scattershot approach to management. When the organizational mission, goals, objectives, and action strategies are articulated and are based upon careful analysis of client needs and environmental realities, then managerial decision-making can be predicated upon hard data with an eye toward future trends. The destination is charted in advance, and decisions can be made to move the organization toward that destination—alert to potential crises, but always focusing on the selected outcome.[10]

Another benefit of planning is the elimination of ignorance—on the part of the clients, the staff, the target markets, and the total organization. Direction, function, and purpose are clearly stated as the planning proceeds, and all parties become knowledgeable about organizational intent. The expectations of all involved groups are clarified, and the relationship between levels of service and funding sources is articulated.[11]

A library that plans for the future has the benefit of knowing where it is going and how it intends to get there. Although no plan allows for every eventuality, the ability to allocate staff and develop a budget based on a written plan means that when changes occur, the library has a document to use for effective decision-making.[12]

The Public Library Development Program

Planning in public libraries in the United States is of fairly recent origin. In 1980, *A Planning Process for Public Libraries*[13] was published as a result of the efforts of the Goals, Guidelines and Standards Committee of the Public Library Association (a division of the American Library Association). This first step toward helping libraries with formal planning was an important building block for the present Public Library Development Program (PLDP).

PLDP has three major components: 1) *Planning and Role Setting for Public Libraries*,[14] describing a step-by-step planning process and introducing the concept of role selection; 2) *Output Measures for Public Libraries* (2d ed.),[15] describing a set of measures to assess common public library services; and 3) the Public Library Data Service, which collects and makes accessible a selective body of information from public libraries across the nation.[16] Public libraries in the United States are currently working with the PLDP components to design planning processes that will, as an additional benefit, generate comparable data.

The original impetus for planning that emerged out of the Public Library Association has evolved into a process that is organic, dynamic, and predicated upon local conditions. A library that engages in a planning effort can be considered proactive, working toward the future by making wise decisions in the present.

IMPERATIVES FOR PLANNING: SELECTING APPROPRIATE ROLES

Traditionally, public libraries in the United States have attempted to be all things to all people. The PLDP manual, by classifying traditional library functions into eight distinct roles, or service profiles, has facilitated the difficult task of setting priorities. Libraries vary in their ability to carry out all eight roles, and communities vary in their needs; therefore, it is critical for management to determine which roles the library will emphasize. Libraries are normally advised to select one or two primary roles and not more than three secondary roles. The following roles have been identified as possible choices:

Community Activities Center. The library is a central focus point for community activities, meetings, and services. It works closely with other community agencies and organizations to provide a coordinated program of social, cultural, and recreational services. The library provides both meeting-room space and equipment for community- or library-sponsored programs such as book talks, speaker series, concerts, art exhibits, tax assistance, voter registration, and so on. The library may create programming for cable television.

Community Information Center. The library maintains a high profile as a clearinghouse for current information on community organizations, issues, and services. It responds to community problems with specialized services, such as a job information center. The library may create local directories, maintain files of local agencies, index local newspapers, participate in community referral networks, and/or maintain a calendar of local events.

Formal Education Support Center. The library assists students of all ages in meeting educational objectives established during their formal courses of study. This assistance may be available to students in elementary and secondary schools, colleges and universities, technical schools, training programs, adult basic education, and continuing education courses. The library offers tours and instructs students in use of the library. It may reserve special materials to meet classroom assignment needs, develop a clearinghouse to identify providers of formal education, or sponsor a literacy program.

Independent Learning Center. The library supports individuals of all ages who are pursuing a sustained program of learning independent of any educational provider. These individuals set their own objectives in such areas as self-improvement, job-related development, hobbies, and cultural interests. The library staff helps these independent students identify an appropriate learning strategy, determine needed resources, and obtain those resources from the library's collection or through interlibrary loan. Continuing, intensive staff involvement with individual learners is a distinguishing characteristic of this role. The library may also function as an educational information center providing occupational counseling or learning/skill inventory tools to help individuals assess their needs. Other services may include a learning exchange, linking learners with others offering to teach a skill, or adult programs on topics of high interest.

Popular Materials Center. The library features and promotes the use of current, high-demand, high-interest materials in a variety of formats for persons of all ages. Merchandising techniques such as face-out shelving, displays, paperbacks near the checkout area, or other "bookstore" strategies may be used. The library may circulate materials at off-site outlets such as shopping malls, community facilities, nursing homes, jails, and so forth.

Preschoolers' Door to Learning. The library encourages preschoolers to develop an interest in reading and learning by providing services both for children alone and for children and parents together. Cooperation with other child-care agencies in the community is ongoing. The library promotes reading readiness from infancy, providing services for self-enrichment and for discovering the pleasures of reading and learning. Services may include programs and materials for infants, for parents and toddlers, and for parents and other adult caregivers (for example, story hours, parenting skills development workshops, reading readiness, and child development).

Reference Library. The library actively provides timely, accurate, and useful information for community residents in their pursuit of job-related and personal interests. The library promotes on-site and telephone reference/information services, ranging from answering practical questions to conducting specialized business-related research to answering questions about government to providing consumer information. The library participates in interlibrary loan and cooperative reference services to obtain information not available locally.

Research Center. The library assists scholars and researchers to conduct in-depth studies, investigate specific areas of knowledge, and create new knowledge. The library's collection is a source of exhaustive information in selected areas. For scholars and other researchers, the library may make special services available, such as assigned carrels and lockers, customized database searching services, or a photocopy center.[17]

Consideration and selection of appropriate roles allow the library to specify the functions it will focus on in order to best serve the community. The decisions should be based upon information that has been secured through a community study. Following the selection of roles and the writing of a mission statement, the planning team sets service priorities, which are subsequently written as goals and objectives. The goals will be phrased as broad statements of intent; the objectives will be measurable or verifiable and time-specific, serving as the basis for evaluation of the library's progress and accomplishments.

In order to implement the goals and objectives, the library staff writes action plans that detail the steps necessary to accomplish each objective. Review of the plan throughout the planning year and final analysis of results complete the planning cycle. Although the written document is vital to library effectiveness, it is the process itself that nurtures communication and growth in concert with community change. This process will be discussed in more detail in chapter 2.

TODAY AND TOMORROW

If the public library is to interact with societal objectives, the mission must be continually defined, articulated, and carried out. Dialogue is required between the professional associational level and the staffs of individual public libraries. This dialogue has been initiated with the introduction of the Public Library Development Program. It must be further nourished and refined, for philosophy is not an idle pastime—it is a foundation and rationale for human endeavor.

Without a "working document" of institutional philosophy of service, there is no guide for establishing operational priorities. Such priorities are particularly crucial in times of economic retrenchment, when the clear guidelines of the "3 Ps"—philosophy, policies, and priorities—can make difficult decisions more manageable and un-derstandable. This is especially true during a period when the "3 national Ps" of power, plentitude, and progress are undergoing serious revision.

With the developments of the last decade, libraries no longer have the luxury of taking their time in responding to societal trends. The public library of today must be proactive in its relationship to society; the reactive posture is no longer tenable.

On a day-to-day basis, questions from both within and without the library concerning products, hours, staffing, and so on cannot be fielded at random, nor with any degree of authority, if institutional priorities are not solidly in place. Further, accountability has become a demand from both legal funders and citizen taxpayers as economic resources become more difficult to allocate. Justification has a hollow ring without a firm—and widely understood—rationale for existence and survival in this fluid society. The mandate for a clearly defined mission and set of roles has been conferred; the public library must respond.

=== ❧ ===

For Discussion

- What evidence is there that the "information age" has affected your community? What future changes do you foresee? How has/can/should your local public library respond to such a fluid environment?
- What is the mission of your public library? Does this mission "fit" with the philosophy of the community?
- Has your library identified its role(s) in the community? If not, what role(s) do you think would be appropriate?
- Is your library engaged in a planning process? If yes, how central to decision-making is this effort? If no, is there any intent to do so?

Scenario One

Of Course the Library Has a Mission—Everybody Knows That!

The Facts

Alpha Public Library serves an unincorporated community of 8,000 people in a rural setting within 100 miles of a well-populated urban/suburban complex.

Beta Public Library, as the metropolitan library for the latter area, claims a potential clientele of 200,000.

Both libraries are located in the same county.

The county government is struggling with significant fiscal problems and does not want to raise taxes in an election year. The plan is to reduce county library funding by approximately 15 percent.

Budget hearings are being held within the next month, at which time the directors of the two libraries will have an opportunity to present their proposed budgets—reflecting fiscal accountability but not necessarily the 15 percent cut—and defend them to the county board.

Several county commissioners are longtime library users and are favorably disposed toward library concerns. Others are avowed fiscal conservatives, determined to cut spending in an effort to hold the line on taxes; library services are not viewed as a high priority.

A hotly debated proposal will also be coming before the county board: the construction of a swimming pool in the metropolitan area, to be partially funded by the county.

What Could/Would Happen If . . .

- Alpha Public Library has a relatively new director who has worked diligently with the board of trustees to develop an institutional mission statement based on identified community needs. Although the one- and five-year plans are not yet complete, they are well under way and strongly support the stated mission.
- Beta Public Library has been experimenting with formal goals and objectives for the past three years. However, only one-year operational documents have been tried thus far. There is a brief statement of library purpose, but the language seems fairly routine and does not appear to relate to the community served.
- Alpha Public Library, as a small agency, has never bothered to define its mission and operates as well as possible on minimal hours, staffing, and funding. Its director is passive, reacting to current conditions.
- The director of Beta Public Library had mobilized committees composed of both staff and community members several years ago to define the library's mission and create a five-year plan. This plan is annually updated, and the yearly operational objectives are a routine spinoff. Community understanding and support of the library is high.
- The Beta Public Library and the Parks and Recreation Department have put together a plan that would create a new complex, consisting of a new library building and a recreation facility containing an indoor/outdoor swimming pool. Petitions have been circulated among the local citizens and neighborhood groups; support for the project is strong.

NOTES

1. Alvin Toffler, *The Third Wave* (New York: Bantam Books, 1981).

2. Charles R. McClure et al., *Planning and Role Setting for Public Libraries: A Manual of Options and Procedures* (Chicago: American Library Association, 1987).

3. Malcolm S. Knowles, *Handbook of Adult Education* (Chicago: Adult Education Association, 1960), 11.

4. Robert Ellis Lee, *Continuing Education for Adults Through the American Public Library, 1833-1964* (Chicago: American Library Association, 1966), 117.

5. Jean B. Wellisch et al., *The Public Library and Federal Policy* (Westport, CT: Greenwood, 1974), 10.

6. Lee, *Continuing Education for Adults*, 77.

7. Doris B. Pagel, "Functions of Public Libraries Toward the Performing of Adult Education Services," Ph.D. dissertation, University of Nebraska, 1977, 42.

8. George A. Steiner, *The "How" of Strategic Planning* (New York: AMACOM, 1978), 3.

9. Darlene E. Weingand, *Marketing / Planning Library and Information Services* (Littleton, CO: Libraries Unlimited, 1987), 11.

10. Ibid., 12.

11. Ibid.

12. *Wisconsin Public Library Standards* (Madison: Wisconsin Department of Public Instruction, 1987), 7.

13. Vernon E. Palmour et al., *A Planning Process for Public Libraries* (Chicago: American Library Association, 1980).

14. McClure et al., *Planning and Role Setting*.

15. Nancy A. Van House et al., *Output Measures for Public Libraries*, 2d ed. (Chicago and London: American Library Association, 1987).

16. The data that will be collected include selected output measures; library descriptors, including role choices; input data, such as holdings, staff, and operating expenditures; and community data, such as population, age distribution, and income.

17. Adapted from McClure, *Planning and Role Setting*, as printed in the *Wisconsin Public Library Standards*, 45-47.

Planning for Change

Once the public library's mission and roles have been formulated, the task and challenge of further developing the planning process can effectively begin. However, an assumption must undergird the entire process: All decisions are written in sand, not stone. This assumption also must be applied to the mission and role statements, for analysis of the library's external and internal environments may indicate that different roles—and hence, a different mission—may be appropriate.

The rationale for engaging in a formal planning process lies in the need to make decisions within an organized framework as opposed to merely coping with and reacting to crises. As the rate of change accelerates, the insistent clamor of problem situations can become deafening, desensitizing management to any activity beyond the immediate present—demand and urgency combine to postpone any thought of tomorrow. Yet the very existence of crisis is a dramatic reason for incorporating the planning process into the range of managerial responsibility. This blending of planning and other managerial functions can be a strong deterrent to the evolution of a crisis; when advance thought and analysis are routine, problems are less likely to grow to crisis proportions.

CRISIS = DECISIONS

The word "crisis" carries a negative connotation in today's society—indeed, it is given synonyms such as "disaster," "emergency," "plight," and "predicament" in my computer's thesaurus. However, the less-often-cited synonyms of "apex" and "climax" are more suited to a positive view. If emotion is removed from a crisis occurrence, these latter two definitions better describe the situation: a series of events that converge and force decisions to be made. Planning and forethought can prevent crippling emotion by providing the opportunity to think through "what ifs" and make tentative decisions before actual crisis points occur. What are some possible catalysts for crisis?

Catalysts for Crisis

One of the very real catalysts for crisis is economic retrenchment. As federal, state, and local funding shrink as sources of library support and as priorities for diminishing community resources undergo shifts and stresses, planning becomes a critical issue.

Another catalyst for crisis occurs when the library administration's posture is reactive instead of proactive. This perspective can be compared to driving a vehicle with the sole purpose of avoiding other vehicles and potential accidents; there is little or no concern for steering a course that will enable smooth and efficient passage toward a desired destination.

A third catalyst for crisis is ignorance: ignorance on the part of the library staff and board regarding library goals and objectives; ignorance of municipal funders to library direction, function, and purpose; ignorance of client groups/taxpayers (both present and potential) as to reasonable expectations of library performance, capabilities, and importance to their lives—particularly in reference to the relationship between levels of service and levels of monetary support.

These catalytic descriptors are almost certain to engender crises. It matters little whether the potential crisis is a day, month, year, or decade away; the seeds are present.

The Two Sides of Events

The curious aspect of crisis is that it reflects but one side of an event—the dark side. The bright side is opportunity. Every possible situation has both a dark and a bright side; it is up to the perceiver to determine which side is dominant.

This reality can be illustrated by a look at the budgetary process. The number of dollars is, in effect, finite in any given year—and frequently controlled by individuals and agencies outside the library's direct control. (Discussion of the considerable effect that library administrations can have on the budget through appropriate marketing strategies is tabled until later in the chapter.) Two approaches to the establishment of the library's budget can be described as follows:

1. The new budget dollar amount will be fixed in one of three ways: 1) at a level comparable to the present fiscal year; 2) to be decreased by X percent; or 3) to be increased by X percent. Whatever the level, the library administration waits to learn the amount of the appropriation and then makes decisions on how the money will be actually apportioned.

2. The library administration uses strategic and operational planning to establish long- and short-range goals and objectives. Based on these established priorities, the administration studies, together with appropriate staff, how these priorities can best be accomplished with the available funds.

Not only are the two approaches and processes different, they produce different outcomes as well. The first is commonly known as the "Band-aid approach," whereas the second is linked to extensive and time-consuming planning—but planning that is cost-effective over the long term.

The Band-aid approach is one of expediency, a patching of a problem rather than a seeking of a long-term solution. In the past, this strategy has frequently worked to some degree, but it is a luxury that is simply no longer viable. Time will be available less often in today's world—and absent from tomorrow's.

A MARKETING APPROACH TO PLANNING

There is a structure to planning, a framework upon which to hang thoughts, ideas, and decisions. The complementary and systematic processes of marketing and planning, when merged, provide a strong and comprehensive structure with which to support the various decision and implementation activities. The schematic for this structure can be found in figure 2.1.

There is an internal logic about the merging of the marketing and planning processes. The Yin and Yang symbol (fig. 2.2) is particularly relevant as a graphic representation of the relationship between the two processes: Although each has intrinsic value, each is incomplete without the other, in the sense that each amplifies the power of the other and provides a wholeness of purpose and application.[1]

In addition, the success rate of each system is directly dependent upon the success rate of the other. Marketing without planning is an exercise; planning without marketing is a formality. The relationship is somewhat analogous to that of theory and practice: Planning sets the conceptual framework; marketing implements the planning directives and creates an environment conducive to an effective exchange process.

The schematic outlined in figure 2.1 provides further explication of how the two systems fit together in practical terms. The clear areas represent elements of the planning process; the shaded areas represent elements of the marketing process. To follow this diagram through, it should be noted that the processes move sometimes in a single direction and, at times, in several directions.

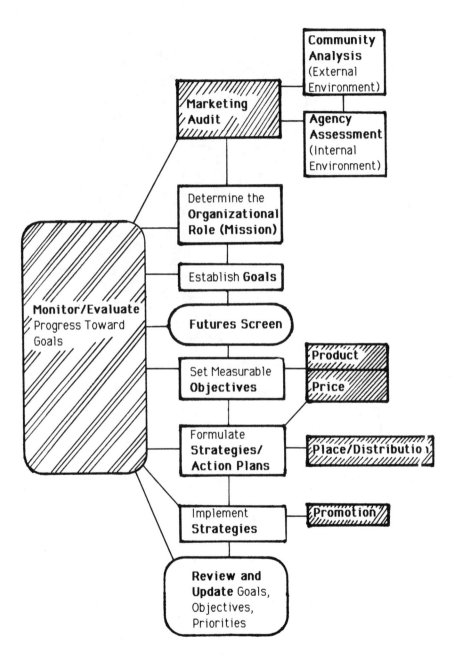

Fig. 2.1. The Combined Planning and Marketing Systems. Originally published in Darlene E. Weingand, *Marketing/Planning Library and Information Services* (Littleton, CO: Libraries Unlimited, 1987).

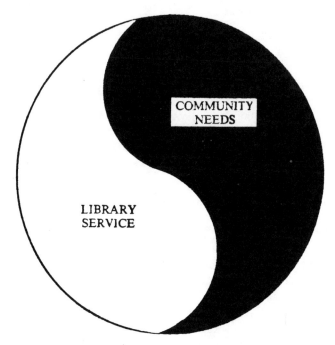

Fig. 2.2. Marketing: The Exchange Relationship.

The following sequence is illustrated in the diagram:

- A community analysis of the library's external environment is conducted.

- An assessment of the library's strengths and weaknesses (internal environment) is made.

- The data from these two assessments become the *marketing audit*.

- Following the marketing audit, the organizational roles and mission are determined.

- Once the mission and roles are determined, the goals for the time period (one and/or five years) are established.

- An analysis of trends is made (a futures screen—see p. 28).

- In order to move toward the established goals, guided by data concerning trends, alternative sets of measurable objectives are created.

- Products (collection, services, programs) are designed in conjunction with the objectives.

- Analysis of price (cost to produce each product) is made to determine product priorities.

- Strategies, or action plans, for each set of objectives are formulated.

- Distribution channels (place) are designed in conjunction with the strategies.

- The strategies are implemented.

- Promotion/communication techniques are designed to implement the strategies.

- A final or summary review and updating is made of all goals, objectives, and priorities. (Note: A process evaluation monitors progress toward the goals throughout the operation of the merged systems.)[2]

Further explanation of each of the elements of this schematic can be found later in this chapter and also in chapter 8. In addition, the reader is directed to *Marketing/Planning Library and Information Services* (Libraries Unlimited, 1987). It is important to emphasize here that integration of the elements of the two processes, as illustrated in the schematic, provides a more reasonable and consistent approach to the marketing and planning efforts than either system employed independently. The elements flow together easily and naturally, allowing a synchronized response to the "where to go" and "how to get there" questions.[3]

BEGINNINGS: THE PLANNING TEAM

This marketing/planning process actually begins with the creation of a planning team (not depicted on the schematic), a working group composed of representatives of those groups that will be affected by the decisions to come. The team should consist of members of the library staff (including the director), policymakers, and funders, plus representatives from business, human service agencies, education, the media, students, parents, older adults, and so forth, depending upon the composition of the community.

There is a very real need for libraries to involve representatives from all levels of the community, as well as all levels of staff, in examining current status and assessing needs.[4] Although community and staff input is frequently sought in typical data gathering, it is less common for such representation to be an integral part of the planning group. Long-range benefits can accrue when those affected by decisions have been involved in making those decisions. The inclusion of a variety of delegates in planning groups not only leads to diverse and realistic perspectives but also develops a sense of "ownership" that can prove most beneficial in the implementation of decisions.

THE PLANNING CYCLE

Once the planning team is formed, there needs to be consideration of how often the process comes full circle and begins to repeat. Under normal conditions, a planning team can expect to work with small circles within a larger circle—individual operational-year planning within the larger context of a five-year long-range plan. Under unusual circumstances, such as a major funding alteration or significant community change, the planning effort may need to be accelerated—particularly in terms of gathering new environmental data.

Operational-year planning is an ongoing process, with the next year's plan beginning to form as soon as the present year is "finalized." (The latter term is in quotation marks in order to emphasize that plans are always inscribed in sand, not stone; plans are always subject to change.) The operational plan is typically tied to the budget development process, and the two processes interact to become the working documents of the library.

The long-range plan, although a five-year projection, has a rolling horizon. Each year, as a new operational planning effort begins, the long-range plan is reviewed and revised as necessary. Therefore, the long-range plan forever extends five years into the future.

A major difference between the marketing/planning approach and other planning systems is the "futures screen," which places considerable emphasis on securing all available data on what may transpire in the next five years and writing objectives to reflect that informed projection. This step typically will mandate three parallel sets of objectives for each goal: 1) an extended set, which assumes an economic climate similar to the present year; 2) a "worst case" set, in which objectives are written to respond to a deteriorating economic picture; and 3) a "blue sky" set, in which possible windfalls and economic upturns are spent in advance!

LEVELS OF EFFORT

One of the unique features of the PLDP approach to planning is consideration of the amount of effort that will be expended. This assessment realistically examines the library's size, budget, and resources and determines the appropriate level of effort to be applied to the planning process. Such an appraisal forestalls the possibility of trying to do too much—which may subsequently create negative staff morale and disinclination toward future planning. The following factors are considered in the determination of level of effort:

- *Participants:* The more individuals and the more groups represented, the higher the library's level of effort for planning.

- *Resources:* Higher levels of effort call for a proportionally greater commitment of the library staff's time and larger expenditures from the library's budget.

- *Library context:* Libraries serving a community with rapid growth or change, a complex and diverse population, shifting economic conditions, or libraries facing a major change in funding may need to plan at a higher level of effort.

- *Planning purposes:* What the library expects the planning process to accomplish may affect the level of effort chosen for some planning phases.

- *Planning structure:* Libraries planning at a basic level of effort may approach many planning activities informally; but as library complexity increases, the planning structure becomes more formal, thus increasing the level of effort.

- *Planning schedule:* Some libraries may complete their first objectives cycle over a very short time period; higher levels of effort may require twelve to eighteen months to complete.[5]

It is important to note that the same level of effort does not have to be present in all phases of the planning process. For example, a major environmental assessment (or marketing audit) may be indicated in Year 1, but not for the next several years.

THE MARKETING AUDIT

Environments, both internal and external, need to be routinely assessed. Three terms are used fairly interchangeably to describe the process that analyzes the client groups to be served: 1) needs assessment; 2) community analysis; and 3) marketing audit. The marketing audit is the umbrella term and encompasses the other terms. Specifically, all three terms can be comparatively defined in the following manner:

1. A *needs assessment* addresses both client expressed (felt) and unexpressed needs, frequently using survey methodology and/or interview techniques to identify those needs.

2. A *community analysis* also examines needs but does so in the context of the whole community picture. Secondary data concerning demographic statistics and growth patterns lend structure to this process, and primary data collection fleshes out the identified parameters.

3. A *marketing audit* covers both the assessment of client needs and the attempt to understand community systems. In addition to this analysis of the external environment, the marketing audit analyzes the internal environment of the library—identifying strengths, limitations and present practice—thereby including the entire environment in its examination. Furthermore, the audit develops a futures screen, which identifies trends and makes projections in both external and internal environments in order to develop contingency plans that will relate to alternative future scenarios.

Kotler defines the marketing audit as a "comprehensive, systematic, independent, and periodic examination of the library's total environment, objectives, strategies, activities, and resources in order to determine problem areas and opportunities and to recommend a plan of action."[6] Almost every word in this definition could be expanded upon and should be considered carefully by the planning team, with particular attention to the process words: "comprehensive," "systematic," "independent," and "periodic."

The library's planning objectives, strategies, activities, and resources (human, fiscal, and physical) are part of its *internal environment*, and a profile of strengths and limitations should be made. Consideration should also be given to organizational climate, communication patterns, organizational structure, and whatever elements of marketing practice are currently in place.

In terms of the *external environment*, the following elements may be appraised:

- *Demographics:* What are the attributes of the community in terms of population, age, gender, educational background, income, employment, and so forth?

- *Geography:* What constitutes the physical landscape, climate, and other physical attributes?

- *Sociology and Psychology:* Who are the individuals and groups that make up the target markets? What are their preferences and biases? What are the social patterns? How do members of the community behave under different sets of circumstances or levels of stress? Can probable behavior be anticipated? Where is the power in the community and how does it flow?

- *Economics:* What is the overall fiscal health of the community? What major businesses/industries are presently in place or about to leave or enter the community? What is the current climate for business and growth?

- *Technology:* What hardware do members of the community presently own or plan to purchase? What is the status of cable television, satellite dishes, computer networks? What use does the business (including farm) community make of different technologies?

- *Politics:* What is the library's relationship to funding sources, both public and private? How does political power flow; how does it relate to societal power? What kinds of lobbying/maneuvering have been done in the past? What worked and what did not?

- *Culture:* What intellectual and artistic activity is present in the community? Are there gaps that the library should attempt to fill? What cooperative ventures could be proposed?

- *Competition:* What agencies, businesses, vendors, organizations, or individuals provide similar products to those offered by the library? What areas of possible cooperation exist? Where do areas of duplication exist? (If the library cannot do it better, faster, or cheaper—and if the market cannot support both the library and the competing agency in this endeavor— then the library should consider reallocating its efforts into more effective pursuits.)

The Marketing Audit as a Management Tool

Before a marketing audit is initiated, certain fundamental points should be considered:

1. As with the planning process, analysis of the environment is not an occasional activity. It must be ongoing so that trends and changing characteristics are detected.

2. It is important that environmental analysis be a collaborative effort among library staff, board members, and representatives of the target markets in the community. It is a learning opportunity for all who are involved and establishes a common base from which they may work together to merge the library into the mainstream of community life. There may be surprises in the data that will alter perceptions of

population demographics, perceived needs, and attitudes toward the library. These surprises will require possible adjustments in expectations, service emphases, and marketing strategies. It is vital that all constituent groups, both internal and external, be involved at the process level, not simply as recipients of a final report.

3. As analysis allows the spotlight to fall on those portions of the community that are unserved, an imperative next step involves outreach efforts that are specifically targeted to those groups. As stated earlier (and often), a major benefit of routine planning and analysis is the monitoring capability that will assess the effectiveness of such outreach efforts. There is a symbiotic relationship between environmental analysis and outreach; maximum effect occurs when these two efforts interact. Although the analysis can admirably sketch in general terms, library service succeeds or falters in terms of its ability to respond to individual human beings with unique perceptions and needs.

4. Change is omnipresent. At no point during the analysis can the data be regarded as static or the coordinate planning be regarded as a rigid progression. Even as the environment is being analyzed, the community is in a state of flux, reacting to political, economic, and social influences. The marketing audit provides snapshots, nothing more. It must be recognized that the task is at once eminently necessary and never completed. This observation is not meant to be discouraging. Rather, it points out the dynamics in which the public library operates. The challenge is to aggressively and positively seek out the avenues for intersection with the community.

The Marketing Audit: A Profile

In order to analyze the library's environments, assets and limitations, a four-step structure can be helpful:

1. *Determine what elements will be covered.* Consider depth of coverage, resources available to conduct the audit, and planning team/staff expectations of anticipated outcomes.

2. *Develop procedures* for collecting data and monitoring the process.

3. *Collect and analyze the data.* Utilize secondary sources first and supplement with primary source data collection where necessary. (Secondary sources consist of data already gathered by other governmental and private agencies. Primary sources provide original data gathered by methods such as interviews or surveys—mail, telephone, or on-site distribution.)

4. *Prepare reports and presentations of the results.* Use both written and oral forms, incorporating summaries and graphics.

Strategies for Collecting Primary Source Data

There are several roads into the external environment that may be traveled; no single method is ideal, and each library must decide upon the most effective strategy for assessing the local situation. Once secondary source information has been exhausted and the planning team has identified gaps in information that need to be addressed, it is both timely and appropriate to consider one or more of the following options. Sampling methodology is generally used to establish an N (number to be surveyed) of reasonable size. Many books on elementary statistics will provide both instruction on sampling procedures and a table of random numbers to use as a base.

The Telephone Survey. The telephone survey is one of the easiest methods to use. Once a sampling pattern is established, the local telephone book can be used as the source of names to be called. However, this method imposes a bias that must be acknowledged: Unlisted numbers are not part of the population to be sampled. A more valid method involves using the computer to randomly generate telephone numbers; many colleges or universities have research labs that are equipped to provide this service.

While the list of people to be surveyed is being prepared, the other part of the task—the design of the interview schedule—should be under way. Questionnaire design is a learned skill; if no staff member has this expertise, exploration of other options is advised—checking with a local college or university for student or faculty assistance; seeking advice from local business personnel; or in some other way locating experienced support from some community resource.

The questionnaire is only as useful as the questions it asks. Before the questionnaire is written, the library administration must determine what it wants to know. Only data required to aid in decision-making should be sought; the temptation to throw in questions because "it would be interesting to know" should be strenuously avoided.

Possible questionnaire elements include: demographic information; usage rate of the library; reasons for nonuse; perceptions of library effectiveness; perceptions of library purpose and function; audiovisual equipment presently owned or plans for purchase; preferred formats/learning styles; and ideas for new or expanded products and methods of distribution.

The Mail Survey. This method differs from the telephone survey in the language used and the structure of the responses. The questions are a bit more formal, as there is no opportunity to question the client's intent—which is possible during the one-on-one interchange of the telephone interview. However, because less human resource time is needed than in the telephone method, a larger sample (N) may be drawn if desired. It must be remembered that tabulation and interpretation of data—regardless of the type of survey method—is a time-consuming process, and personnel may need to be recruited and/or trained if effective analysis is to be done.

The Interview. Another approach entirely is the in-person interview of library users (in the library), members of the general community (on the street or house-to-house), or both. This method is staff time-intensive, in that a designated—and trained—staff member (paid or unpaid) conducts each in-depth interview, but the opportunity to gather individualized information can have unique benefits. Many attitudes and perceptions may emerge that would not have surfaced in a simple questionnaire format. The personal interview can be a treasure hunt. Although interviews should be standardized, with a set of prescribed questions being asked of each interviewee, the ensuing conversation may take unexpected turns, and the alert interviewer may secure valuable unsolicited information as a by-product. In addition, the one-to-one interaction can give interviewees a sense that the library is interested in and cares about citizens' opinions.

Because of the time involved, the personal interview technique utilizes a much smaller sample (N), and less of a cross-section of the community is consulted.

The Focus Group. An expansion of the interview is the focus group. A small group of invited participants (with knowledge, experience, or interest in predetermined areas) is gathered to explore needs and options under the guidance of a trained facilitator. No interview schedule of questions is prepared; rather, the facilitator begins with broad, general questions and leads the group to focus more and more tightly on specifics as the exercise progresses. This method can be extremely helpful in charting future directions and gathering data for decision-making.

The Community Meeting. The community meeting is not suggested as a means of reaching the indifferent citizen or the nonuser. Participants in such a meeting or hearing should be regarded as "interested parties" because they have made the effort to attend. Once participants have assembled, the following procedure may be used to structure the event:

1. *Introductions*—A sharing among members of the group, which may include names, addresses, occupations, and/or other information that may be of significance in a particular community.

2. *Brainstorming*—The proposing of ideas in rapid succession with no judgment or evaluation of their merit. Ideas may incorporate citizen concerns, needs, wishes, hopes, and dreams for library service and operation. A designated recorder lists all ideas on

large newsprint pads, taping completed sheets around the room. Formal nominal group methodology may prove to be useful at this stage.

3. *Social period*—An opportunity for participants to discuss proposed ideas informally over coffee. During this time, the recorder arranges (and recopies) the suggestions into logical categories—funding, hours of service, service to target markets, use of technology, etc.

4. *Discussion*—A collective sharing of opinions by the reassembled group.

5. *Ranking*—The final step, in which the group members, either together through discussion or independently on paper, rank the suggestions in priority order. (A "quick and dirty" method is for all participants to select their "favorite five" from each category.) The recorder tallies all responses and indicates the top vote-getters. (Note: In communities where interactive cable TV or community computer bulletin boards are available, an alternative possibility for this step would be to allow citizens to provide input electronically. This approach would add depth to the exercise and encourage wider participation.)

It should be noted that a combination of these methods may be effective. The individual library administration must decide what seems both reasonable and appropriate to the local situation.

The Marketing Audit and Political Savvy

The library has historically been promoted as a package: an efficient, convenient, and protective wrapping of information insulating the user and isolating both the information and the librarian. The quiet and hallowed stacks provide comfort and solace to the bibliophile and a sense of rightness and order to the librarian. The mystique of hushed learning is a salvation to the earnest scholar—but a barrier to many casual seekers of information.

These old concepts of packaging focus on the institutional aspects of library operations and continually emphasize the image of the library as a building, a physical structure housing and preserving the records of knowledge. This image has a decreasing validity in today's world, and those who seek to nourish it as an exclusive or primary model are doing a disservice to the library's effectiveness—indeed, are threatening its very survival in the information age.

The library can be viewed either in its "institutional" role as the storehouse of a product with intrinsic value or as a point of intersection between human need and relevant data.[7] If the desired outcome of library service is the satisfaction of user needs, it seems reasonable to propose that knowledge about the potential library user is essential to library planning and operations.

Is the public library a building containing resources of sufficient value that a majority of the population will both utilize it and support its operation? Multiple research studies indicate that this is decidedly not the case, that public libraries are frequently used by a minority of the population. As for economic support, the level of funding for public agencies is ever under challenge; fiscal constraints and budget cuts are more the rule than the exception.

The public library competes with other agencies for each dollar of tax support. If the library is not to come in a poor second to such "basic" or "essential" services as police and fire protection, garbage collection, and snow removal, the library's services must also be regarded as "essential." How can this be accomplished? Certainly, the traditional posture of guarding a cherished product can no longer suffice; public awareness of the library's value has not been sufficiently demonstrated. Because access to information is a survival and coping strategy in today's world, it seems reasonable to suggest that the library—as the access channel to information—may be viewed as fully "essential." In order to foster this perception, an active—and interactive—attitude needs to be an integral part of public library mission and operations.

Library professionals who suffer from a lack of political awareness and savvy may regard the activities of a marketing audit as a frivolous use of staff time. They may, once the research is done, file the results away without realizing the potential benefits of such research for decision-making and political influence.

There is little strength in the presentation of administration-perceived needs and wants to funding authorities, but there is much power in the accurate substantiation and documentation of library requirements by data reflecting community needs. Information truly is power. Public libraries have historically been less astute than other segments of the political structure in learning to manipulate the channels and sources of power. This naiveté can no longer be afforded. The marketing audit is a valuable ally in the struggle toward parity of power.

CHARTING A NEW DIRECTION

Once the environmental data have been gathered through the marketing audit, the library's mission will need to be reassessed. It is not uncommon for the new data to suggest that the mission and roles that are in place, even if only informally articulated, are no longer totally relevant to community needs. This potential disparity, of course, is one of the implicit side-effects of seeking community input—and the library must be prepared to respond to what is learned. Indeed, it can be more damaging to ask for community input and then ignore it, than never to ask at all. Once the data are collected, the library has a duty to analyze and synthesize the results in order to inform decision-making.

The revised mission and roles statements lend substance and form to the process that follows: the development of goals, objectives, and action statements.

DEVELOPING GOALS, OBJECTIVES, AND ACTION STATEMENTS

Goals can be defined as aspirations—statements of purpose or intent written in global terms. They may or may not be attainable (i.e., when would one achieve "effective information service"?), but they serve as a focus for directed activity.

Based on this definition, it can be seen that goals, although fluid, are reasonably constant; at the same time, well-written goals frequently adapt well to changing situations. Library goals are prime movers for library policy, together with the established mission and roles statements. It is from the goals that practical and measurable objectives can be extrapolated—objectives that serve as the road map for library operations.

Objectives are statements of purpose or intent that are both measurable and attainable and that move the library toward a stated goal. If "effective information service" is a goal, a related objective might be: "To establish an information and referral service by May 19." Objectives are tools; more important, they are tools that can relate closely to changing environments. The development of parallel sets of contingency objectives (see the section on "Futures Screens" below) creates working documents that can be referred to regardless of changes in current conditions. These alternative sets provide thoughtfully considered decisions regarding foreseen—but not yet real—situations. Moreover, the very existence of alternative objectives maintains the proactive state; no matter how severe the crisis, the potential waste of reactive response is preempted.

The development of *action statements* is the final step in the implementation phase of the planning process. Each objective, in order to be accomplished, requires a series of completed actions. These actions are both concrete and detailed, usually listed in sequential order. Like objectives, they are measurable, contain a time line, and denote who is responsible for their completion. Examples of action statements to correlate with the sample objective of establishing an information and referral service might include:

- "To establish a special area in the library for information and referral by February 19. Responsibility: Director"

- "To hire/train a specialist in I&R service by March 19. Responsibility: Assistant Director"

- "To create an initial community information file by May 19. Responsibility: I&R Specialist"

In other words, action statements provide the working outline of specific tasks that must be executed before the objective is realized.

THE FUTURES SCREENS

It is imperative that "futures screens"—considerations of alternative futures—are injected into the planning process. In past years, when a typical community analysis was done, the concern was usually centered on the present, with little or no thought of what rapid change might dictate. It is the responsibility of the planning team to keep up to date on trends and probabilities that may impact upon library operations and to use this information as a screen to filter the collected data. Part of this currency should result from the marketing audit, as data should be secured from city and county planning authorities.

However, the planning team must also shoulder the responsibility of interpretation. For example, if an emerging cable TV system will allow 24-hour access to the library's catalog and reference service, a skeleton round-the-clock staff may be desirable—with reduced hours for the library building—even though the marketing audit results may suggest that the community wishes the library to be open more hours per week. The interpretation of what constitutes "more hours per week" is critical here, and the information concerning CATV access certainly suggests an entirely different approach and response to that perceived need.

Once library goals are determined, another futures screen drops into place. This screen filters goal statements through alternative scenarios (or descriptions of possibilities). Parallel sets of objectives are written so that the library continues to work toward established goals, regardless of external changes. These three sets of objectives for each goal address the following situations:

- Conditions (economic, societal, political, etc.) remain similar to the present.

- Conditions change markedly in a positive direction.

- Conditions change markedly in a negative direction.

In the case of funding alone, it can easily be seen that these three vastly different scenario possibilities might prompt objectives that would vary widely. It should be noted that time is a significant variable here; projections for one year can be far more explicit and probable than projections for five years. Yet both one- and five-year plans must be constructed if effective proactive planning is to occur. The result of filtering through futures screen #2 would be multiple sets of measurable objectives for each goal.

The Use of Forecasting Techniques

Just as in the marketing audit, in which both secondary and primary sources have value, projections for use in futures screens can also be developed using secondary and primary means. Secondary sources might include city or county planning commission data and projections from other agencies, corporations, or institutions. Primary data are always more time-consuming to obtain, but if administration or staff have interest in this area, the results can be rewarding.

Forecasting techniques are becoming useful and needed tools within the planning process. Many specific techniques have been created and validated. Some of these include:

Contextual mapping

Force analysis

Relevance trees

Delphi technique

Cross impact matrix

Scenarios

Ariole, a planning guide

Decision matrix technique

Morphological analysis

Technology assessment

Trend analysis

Bayesian statistics

Markov chain theory

Monte Carlo techniques[8]

Each technique employs quantitative and/or qualitative skills that can be as pertinent for their purposes as statistical measures have proved to be in the analysis of numerical data. Fluency in both types of research strategies is important to the process of planning. Large libraries frequently have the resources to hire or train a staff member in these areas of expertise. Smaller agencies will need to select or modify existing techniques to a scale that is comfortable and appropriate to their needs and recruit volunteers with the capability to assist.

What is important is that forecasting be incorporated into planning; that alternative scenarios for future events be drawn in an effort to plan for contingencies; and that the use of forecasting techniques be viewed not with skepticism or dread but with hope and the positive attitude that such strategies may open a window where none existed before.

The process of preparing for change, which incorporates both planning and marketing elements, is more than a sum of these parts. When the intent of the effort is the marriage of excellent products with client need and a proactive attitude, the library has every probability of achieving the desired relationship of mutual benefit between itself and the community. It is to this end that planning for change aspires.

For Discussion

- What crises can occur in a community? What kinds have occurred in your community in the past five years?
- Were these crises viewed as problems or opportunities? If problems, what opportunity factors can you identify?
- In your community, whom would you put on the planning team?
- What level of effort is possible for your library to expend in a planning process?
- In terms of the internal environment, what are your library's strengths and limitations?
- Using the factors listed in the chapter, describe the external environment within which your library operates.
- When your library planning team begins to gather data for the marketing audit, what secondary sources are available in your community? within your library? What agencies can provide data regarding future trends?
- What method or methods would you recommend to gather primary data?

Scenario Two
The Staff Is Too Busy to Plan

The Facts

The Geranium Public Library serves a community of 40,000 people in a suburban location.

Most residents are blue-collar workers in a local automotive plant.

Library services and collection reflect the average educational level of the community.

The library has never done a planning process because the staff is so busy.

The following events occur within a two-year time period:

- A research park is established and a biotechnology firm and other research groups begin to move their headquarters into the complex.
- Many professional and highly educated newcomers move into town.
- Local schools are overloaded and some local tax monies are diverted to building expansion.
- Additional apartments and condominiums are quickly erected to accommodate the influx of employees in the new research park.
- An economic recession forces the automotive plant to close down operations.
- Library circulation increases by 200 percent.

What Could/Would Happen If . . .
- The library does not engage in a formal planning process.
- The library begins to plan, but representatives of the community are not in the planning group.
- The library is immersed in its first planning process but has not considered using futures screens or otherwise monitoring trends.
- A complex, time-consuming community analysis was well under way when the announcement of the research park was made.
- Consideration of staff time and resources has led to a scaled-down needs assessment procedure.
- The city and county planning commissions were consulted as part of the marketing audit.
- Write your own conditions.

NOTES

1. Darlene E. Weingand, *Marketing/Planning Library and Information Services* (Littleton, CO: Libraries Unlimited, 1987), 16.

2. Ibid., 18.

3. Ibid., 20.

4. Carlton Rochell, *Wheeler and Goldhor's Practical Administration of Public Libraries*, rev. ed. (New York: Harper & Row, 1981), 23.

5. Charles R. McClure et al., *Planning and Role Setting for Public Libraries: A Manual of Options and Procedures* (Chicago: American Library Association, 1987), 4.

6. Philip Kotler, *Marketing for Nonprofit Organizations* (Englewood Cliffs, NJ: Prentice-Hall, 1982), 185.

7. Brenda Dervin, "Useful Theory for Librarianship: Communication, Not Information," *Drexel Library Quarterly*, 13:3 (July 1977), 16-32.

8. Stephen P. Hencley and James R. Yates, *Futurism in Education: Methodologies* (Berkeley, CA: McCutchan, 1974).

Focus on the Client

In the effort to create a relationship of partnership between a library and its clients, the focus of product design and distribution must necessarily be placed upon the client. The atmosphere that is most nurturing to library growth and excellence is one of mutual benefit—clients actively support the library because they perceive that it is essential to their quality of life.

Moreover, there is a natural correlation between serving clients in the public library and understanding human needs and development. Adding emphasis on the human dimension of library service helps to create the bonding of mutual benefit stated above that is so essential to vitality and progress. When library service is client-centered, it moves well beyond the traditional scenario focusing on librarian/question and toward the more desired scenario of librarian/client. In addition, when the heuristic approach is plugged into this interchange, the many additional facets of human personality and experience transform the exchange and require a far more in-depth treatment.

CREATING A CLIENT-CENTERED APPROACH

"Mirroring" was successfully used by psychologist Carl Rogers as a technique to facilitate this centering on the client. This technique consists primarily of a rephrasing of client statements, such as, "If I am understanding correctly, you are looking for. . . ." This approach has advantages in that it verifies that the person in the professional/-helper role understands the meaning and intent of the client's statement, and it offers the client an opportunity to affirm, clarify, change, or restructure the original statement. "Mirroring" is based on certain basic concepts:

- The client is motivated in positive directions; the client is rational and socialized and to a large extent determines self-destiny.

- The total individual is considered; alteration of any part may produce changes in any other part.

- The personality is always in a state of development, and all human behavior hinges on the motive of self-actualization.

- Reality is what is perceived as reality.[1]

In relating to a client, therefore, there are fundamental conditions that need expression: unconditional positive regard from others; self-regard and valuing from the client; genuineness of the helper; a minimum state of client anxiety; psychological contact—a relationship—between helper and client; and client perception that these conditions are in effect.[2]

The implications for the librarian/helper are clear: The creation of the environment, or conditions for helping and learning, is a significant responsibility and challenge, but one that is well worth the effort.

"But," the cry may ring out, "how can anyone hope to devote the time and energy that this in-depth service would require?" It is true, of course, that every client encounter will not demand such depth. Many reference questions are elementary or directional in nature, and minimum attention need be paid. The professional librarian should, however, be qualified and competent to assess, through the reference interview, what level of professional expertise needs to be tapped. This is where the art and science of librarianship merge in the pursuit of excellence.

DEVELOPMENTAL THEORIES

The public library, in order to reach its goal of full and effective service for its clients, needs to be staffed with personnel who have deep interest and caring insight into the ever-fluid aspects of human development. The library's clients are not a homogeneous mass but rather a potpourri of personalities with a wide range of individual differences and experiences.

Psychologists have repeatedly conducted studies on human behavior in an effort to explain it, and many separate theories have been advanced. The first step in this examination of theories is to acknowledge that everyone is a theorist. We may disguise our theories as common sense, proverbs, or slogans—but theories they remain. The next logical step is to admit that our theories are frequently untested and hence must be viewed as unverified conjecture. When the focus of speculation is the human being, however, it is important that those perspectives that have emerged via scientific investigation be given major consideration.

There are several major approaches to understanding human development. A discussion of these approaches follows.[3]

The Psychoanalytic Perspective

The psychoanalytic approach is related to the work of Sigmund Freud and his followers. It is concerned with negative and abnormal aspects of behavior and postulates that early life experiences determine total personality development. The premise of an unconscious mental life is a major assumption.

Freud's sexually described stages of development are fairly well known; the progression represents the transformation of the human being from the totally egocentric infant to the reality-oriented adult. Briefly, these stages are:

1. The oral stage, in which satisfaction and discomfort associated with oral activities set the framework for the adult's capacity to cooperate and share.

2. The anal stage, in which the trait of autonomy is either forged or blunted.

3. The phallic stage, in which the foundation for self-confidence, ambition, and curiosity is laid.

4. The Oedipus conflict, the successful resolution of which sets the pattern for healthy sexual identity.

5. The latency period, which serves as a time for establishing standards and values.

6. The genital stage, which, in this perspective, serves as the capstone and completes the development of the healthy sexual adult.

Implications for library service predicated on the assumptions of this theoretical perspective would include the following:

- Problems, rather than potential, are the focus of this perspective; rather than concentrating on present and future needs, this theory stresses the remediation of deficiencies.

- Caretakers of children (including librarians and teachers) are held accountable for aspects of psychological development; this is a one-way view, with little emphasis on interaction effects or on the child's own responsibility for learning and growth.

- There is little or no margin allowed for the exercise of choice and free will; this aspect of the theory negates individual opportunity for change.

- Finally, the concern is with what not to do rather than on what to do.

Freudian psychology is a powerful influence, but its essentially dark perspective can be unattractive to those library personnel who seek to provide a challenging, dynamic environment in which individual growth can flower.

The Behaviorist Perspective

Behaviorists claim that psychology is the study of behavior as viewed through systematic and controlled observation. In addition, behaviorists frequently extrapolate from the study of animal behavior.

One of this perspective's major premises is that human development is overwhelmingly a function of learning and experience within the context of the person's environment. In an effort to quantify data and results, studies are frequently conducted in terms of simple situations and behaviors—and often in a laboratory situation where individual variables can be manipulated. The concept of reinforcement of learning, as both a strong support to and an intrinsic element in the learning process, is critical to this theory. Finally, these specifics are generalized into universal principles applicable to behavior.

Implications for library service center around learning sequences rather than developmental stages. Because learning is a core concept in this perspective, the origins and conditions under which learning takes place are of prime importance. Therefore, the library environment—a potpourri of sound and silence, materials and machines, reference and referral, information and ideas—becomes a significant factor in effective service.

Competence, or observable and measurable behavior, is recognized as a true indicator of knowledge and expertise. This recognition affects collection development, fostering continuing education opportunities and an attitude toward staff development and lifelong learning that facilitates conditions for growth.

The Humanist Perspective

In the humanistic perspective, the concern is with potential, unique capabilities, and dignity—with a dash of joy to add zest. The study of impulsive behavior and/or reaction gives way to recognition of rational decision-making and intent. Internal and self-directed tendencies—not external influences—are paramount. This view implies that individuals are basically self-determining, responsible, and proactive in their developmental process, and there is a fundamental conviction that each person is unique and capable of excellence. Two basic life conflicts are identified in this theoretical perspective: 1) the propensity toward pleasure/love versus the satisfaction of achieving decisive real-world commitments and responsibilities; and 2) the search for security versus the urge for adventure and creative action.

This optimistic and sympathetic view of human development is perhaps the most comfortable for human service professionals, which include library personnel. The assumptions allow and encourage interaction with library clients on a positive, growth-stimulating plane where the permutations of the human personality are nurtured and options for an expanded quality of life can be explored.

The one-on-one relationship between librarian and client, which is the norm in library service, fits in well with this vision of unique individuality; however, perfunctory service and response to client requests are decidedly out of place because they deny the three-dimensional aspects of human intellect and emotion. Librarians who identify most closely with this theory of development need to examine their methods of clinical practice to determine whether there is true congruence between their belief system and their style of service.

Developmental Stage Theory

In addition to major perspectives on human development, there are various theories of developmental stages—that is, the belief that life is divided into qualitatively different and sequential periods, each stage building upon its predecessor. Some theorists hold that one stage must be completely worked through before the next stage can be entered. Others assert that although stages are indeed sequential, one can pass developmentally through this progression—but ultimately must return to those stages that were left unfinished.

Freudian stages were briefly described earlier in the chapter. A second major stage theorist, Jean Piaget, suggested four major periods of intellectual development:

1. Sensorimotor period (birth to 2 years—stimulation and manipulation)

2. Preoperational thought period
   - classification by single salient features (2-4 years—pre-operational phase)
   - classification in terms of relationships (4-7 years—intuitive phase)

3. Period of concrete operations (7-11 years—ability to use logical operations)
   - reversibility (arithmetic)
   - classification (organization into hierarchies)
   - seriation (organization into ordered series)

    4. Period of formal operations (11-15 years—abstract thinking; hypothesis-testing)[4]

Another stage theorist worth noting is Erik Erikson,[5] who visualized eight successive stages of personality development. Each stage is described in terms of a positive trait versus a negative trait. However, the concept of the continuum is applicable here, as it is unlikely that any person would be positioned at either the positive or negative extreme. Hopefully, as maturation occurs, movement occurs along the continuum toward the positive end. Once again, the age ranges listed are simple descriptors, and actual examples of development may vary. The eight stages include:

1. Trust vs. Mistrust (birth-1 year)

2. Autonomy vs. Shame/Doubt (2 years)

3. Initiative vs. Guilt (3-5 years)

4. Industry vs. Inferiority (6 years-puberty)

5. Identity vs. Identity/Role Confusion (puberty)

6. Intimacy vs. Isolation (20-30 years)

7. Generativity vs. Stagnation (middle age)

8. Integrity vs. Despair (retirement)

Though Piaget addresses the intellectual side of the three-dimensional person, the human personality completes the total picture. Library services and materials that are concerned with psychology, values, and ethics can be most useful in facilitating growth. The public library has a definite role in assisting human potential.

These are but a few of the stage theorists. Roger Gould, Daniel Levinson, George Vaillant, and Bernice Neugarten offer well-thought-out models and perspectives, and a popular treatment of stage theory can be found in Gail Sheehy's *Passages*. (See "Suggestions for Further Reading" at the end of the book.)

As a summary to this discussion of stage theories, Robinson's synthesis of many of the elements proposed by these theorists in terms of adult development can be useful. His composite can be summarized as follows:

Early Adulthood: Intimacy vs. Isolation
  • Ages 18-22: Pulling Up Roots—the transition from adolescence to adulthood and establishment of a life on one's own; educational preparation, beginning work, establishing a home, managing time and money

- Ages 22-28: Becoming Adult—becoming autonomous; setting in motion life patterns; selecting a mate, beginning a career, owning a home, becoming a parent; believing one can do anything

- Ages 28-33: Catch-30—characterized by second thoughts, feelings of restrictions in career, marriage, relationships; a time of change and dissatisfaction; urges to make new choices; time of reappraisal, putting down roots, searching for values

Middle Adulthood / Middle Age: Generativity vs. Stagnation
- Ages 33-38: Becoming One's Own Person—rooting and extending, developing competence, establishing a niche in society, working at "making it"; conflicting time demands

- Ages 38-46: Midlife Transition—often unstable and explosive, similar to adolescence; reassessment of marriage and career; relating to adolescent children and aging parents; a search for meaning; reversal between men and women (women becoming more career-oriented, men becoming more nurturing and home-oriented); vulnerability to extramarital affairs, substance abuse, overeating, divorce, suicide

- Ages 46-53: Settling Down—formation of a new life structure; commitment to new choices; discovery of ultimate aloneness and responsibility for self

- Ages 53-60: Renewal or Resignation—self-acceptance, realism, and warmth; increased personal happiness and satisfaction; a time of resignation if midlife passage not dealt with successfully; development of secondary interests in anticipation of retirement

Later Adulthood: Integrity (belief in life's purpose) vs. Despair
- Ages 60-65: Late Adult Transition—retirement and dread or anticipation . . . especially difficult for those self-defined in terms of careers; adjustment to lower income; confrontation of loss (job, home, spouse); sense of powerlessness, isolation, meaninglessness—or a heightened sense of challenge and growth

- Ages 65 and up: Late Adulthood—engaging the phases of retirement; correlation between educational activity and self-concept, zest for living; increase in religious feelings and beliefs; search for meaning of life; the process of dying[6]

The work of these various stage theorists can be extrapolated to the library setting in terms of reference, collection development, and programming efforts—at every level of interaction with each client. When library service is correlated to approximate client developmental status, the results can be more positive and effective. (It must be understood, however, that the ages given are only estimations and that individual development varies widely.)

THE ADULT AS LIFELONG LEARNER

Moving one step beyond stage theory, yet certainly using it as a foundation block, are the various assumptions of "andragogy." Andragogy—the art and science of helping adults learn—was proposed and developed by Malcolm Knowles[7] and bridges several theories and perspectives, providing a composite picture of adult behavior and characteristics. Adult learners may be described as:

- *Ready to learn.* The movement is toward social and occupational competence and away from psychological developmental factors. Librarians need to assist learners in filling knowledge gaps; the attitude that no questions are "stupid" and that inquiry leads to opportunity is critical to effective library service.

- *Caught climbing the mountain of time.* To the young, time is infinite; somewhere in the middle adult years the perspective changes, and time is viewed as finite and increasingly precious. Librarians should be sensitive to this evolving perspective. Not every adult wishes to learn research skills. For many, time is more valuable than money, and cash exchanged for information is considered fair and just. Librarian-produced information, whether for a fee or for free, is desirable to a significant number of clients.

- *Problem-centered in orientation to learning.* Motivation is directly related to the solution of today's problems, and experiential activities are the most enduring. Librarians need to focus on the learner and the learning process, rather than on sterile materials. A shift in emphasis from facts to people brings strength and purpose to library operations. The stress on today's concerns and problems relates learning to reality and binds both into a motivational framework that works.

- *Self-directed.* Adults view themselves as capable and independent, competent to direct and evaluate their own learning. Librarians need to treat adults as being genuinely self-directed. The tendency to project authority and enforce a variety of "shoulds" must give way to the scenario of the librarian as a learning resource seeking to meet learner needs through a collegial and collaborative relationship.

- *Experienced in life skills.* The adult's years of experience are incorporated into the learning process, and mistakes are viewed as opportunities for learning. Librarians can capitalize on this treasure trove of experience by incorporating it into the resource scenario. To reject this life experience is equivalent to rejecting the client as a person and must be avoided.

What does all this mean? There are definite library service applications, but there is, in addition, an overriding concept: that the librarian's degree of effectiveness in interacting with clients is directly correlated to the depth of his or her understanding of the developmental process. Although the various approaches to the examination of human development are not in total agreement, there are many overlapping areas where a degree of consensus is reached. However, consensus—or its lack—does not negate the significance of the individual perspectives and theories. Every candle that helps to shed light upon the human condition adds to the overall illumination, and benefits cannot help but accrue.

Librarians who are truly interested in meeting client needs will study these crude maps and chart the courses of service that seem most likely to reach the desired destinations. Human development is complex, perplexing, and challenging. Effective library service can be an invaluable aid to both client self-understanding and societal progress toward the common good.

Lifelong Learning: A Mandate in a Changing Society

When the mission of the public library in society is pondered, the trio of education, information, and recreation is frequently injected glibly into conversation. The historical confusion over mission has usually revolved around these terms—sometimes playfully, but often in earnest. The development of a spectrum of roles, from which the library is to select the most appropriate to the local situation, has produced both confusion and clarification in the awareness of options and the need for setting priorities.

Accordingly, today's cultural awareness and use of language have produced the term "lifelong learning"—a combination of jargon and vision, to be sure, but a concept worthy of serious consideration. This consideration can be particularly productive if the concepts of public library mission and lifelong learning can be effectively and validly joined in terms of improving the quality of life.

Monroe developed a view of the public library as a learning center structured on a mission continuum. Points of intersection on this continuum, beginning with the most conservative, may include:

- Supporting learning through provision of requested materials

- Serving as a support system for other organizations, institutions, and agencies

- Serving as a multimedia community learning center

- Identifying significant community problem situations

- Participating through materials and services as part of a community problem-solving task force[8]

This last, most liberal position places the public library in the role of infusing information into the decision-making process—a decidedly proactive stance. All of these positions can be blended into one or more of the PLDP-recommended roles for public libraries.

With the movement away from linear life patterns and toward diversity of lifestyles, public libraries have a distinct opportunity to offer random access to learning and to serve as a hub for these shifting models of behavior. This perspective implies that learning will come to be viewed as legitimate in any location where stimulating resources can be found. Further, learning will be seen as a process within the learner rather than as a product related to specific credential-granting providers. Learning will be a coping skill needed to survive the vagaries of change, a necessary ingredient in the totality of the life cycle, and a stimulus to heighten the quality of life.

This view of learning is not a fantasy but a trend that is already in place and evolving in tandem with the impact of change. Credit-by-examination is granted by most colleges and universities; competency-based education, experiential learning, and learning contracts that relate to the goals of the learner are becoming more common modes of educational structure. The role of the public library in the midst of this flux is not fully formed, but the possibilities are as varied as the creative imagination will allow.

TOMORROW'S LITERACY
AND TODAY'S CHILD

Literacy has many faces. It can be defined as cultural memory, the ability to apply yesterday's heritage to today's problems; it can be viewed as critical analysis of all forms of media; and, probably the most common use today, it can be perceived as the ability to read and understand printed material. In reference to this latter perspective, Jonathan Kozol asserts that the United States ranks forty-ninth among 158 member nations of the United Nations in literacy.[9] He further states, in a chapter entitled "The Pedagogic Time Bomb: The Children of Nonreaders," that illiteracy is not a new phenomenon in the United States. By any standard there were many more illiterate Americans 100 years ago—and perhaps as recently as 1960. In the past two decades, the number of those who cannot read at all has either diminished slightly or remained unchanged. It is functional illiteracy which has increased; this is the case because this term is, in itself, a "function" of the needs imposed upon a person by the economic and the social order. The economy and the society have changed in every age. It is the rate of change, and the degree to which it may outpace the literacy level of the nation, that determine what part of that nation is unable to survive and to prevail within the context of its times. The speed-up in the rate of change, especially within the past two decades, is well known.[10]

Kozol's emphasis on the rate of change must be echoed here. His observations also serve to reinforce the focus on change in chapter 2. But beyond these often acknowledged changes in the economic and social order, there are also changes in values, technologies, and the needs related to coping strategies. Kozol's chapter heading referring to "children of nonreaders" provides food for thought and directly relates to the "why" of illiteracy. When adults are nonreaders, the role modeling for the enjoyment of reading as an intellectual and recreational activity is missing. Therefore, as libraries pick up the challenge posed by literacy issues, it seems imperative that adults and children together engage in the pursuit of print literacy as a means of learning to cope, as a source of shared pleasure, and as a very real mutual reinforcement.

The National Commission on Excellence in Education explicitly draws connections between adults and children, stating that

> your right to a proper education for your children carries a double responsibility. As surely as you are your child's first and most influential teacher, your child's ideas about education and its significance begin with you. You must be a living example of what you expect your child to honor and to emulate. Moreover, you bear a responsibility to participate actively in your child's education. . . . Monitor your child's study; encourage good study habits; encourage your child to take more demanding rather than less demanding courses. . . . Be an active participant in the work of the schools. Above all, exhibit a commitment to continued learning in your own life.... Children will look to their parents and teachers as models of such virtues.[11]

There are very real benefits and connections between lifelong learning, literacy skills, and the building of tomorrow through the efforts of today. These benefits and connections are best viewed in the context of partnership between adults, children, and library staff.

ADVANTAGES FOR LIBRARY STAFF

The benefits to clients of public library involvement as an active partner in lifelong learning are many and varied. But what of the often overlooked benefits to library staff?

Departure from familiar duties and procedures affects people in as many ways as there are human personalities. Reactions can range from profound dismay to wholehearted enthusiasm. The following positive aspects can provide an enriching environment for the workplace:

- The stimulation of working with clients in their learning endeavors can be profound and carry over to other professional responsibilities.

- The personal satisfaction gained from the process of helping people learn can be more inspiring than routine provision of materials.

- The opportunity to assist learners in an advising/counseling capacity can be both challenging and rewarding.

- The hesitation common to staff without adequate skills to function in this arena can be dispelled with appropriate continuing education opportunities. There is potential resentment inherent in significant new ventures, and this reality needs to be addressed by the library administration and countered with adequate in-service training. Newness is an intrinsic part of change, and staff reluctance to risk and experiment will seriously hamper library involvement in this world of change. Conversely, positive staff engagement in the process of change has a spillover effect into other areas of library operations.

There is no question that the public library has a definite and unique role to play in enabling citizens to achieve the improved quality of life they desire. Further, the social and vocational world today's youths are being prepared for may not exist when they become adults.[12]

Lifelong learning can be the framework that provides the library with a structure for its mission and the citizenry with the fullest possible development in the successive stages of life. The responsibility of the public library to the community is beyond real comprehension and must not be taken lightly.

=========================== ❧ ===========================

For Discussion

- How can "mirroring" help the library staff work with clients?
- How can an understanding of "stage theories" help librarians to better serve their clients?
- How can lifelong learning benefit the individual? the community?
- Of the several definitions of literacy, which one(s) are addressed by your library? How could the others be incorporated into library programming?
- On a scale of 1 to 5, where does your library place in focusing on the client?

1_____2_____3_____4_____5
Little focus   Totally focused

Scenario Three

The Library Is in Existence Because . . .

The Facts

Librarians Anna and Greg were hired to provide public services in an urban library serving a population of 50,000.

Greg brings a conservative and traditional philosophy of library service to the position, emphasizing the "warehouse" perspective and comprehensive collection development. He sees the library's mission as one of curator of knowledge.

Anna perceives the library's mission as one of service to people; materials are important, but only insofar as they respond to client needs. Because of this emphasis on people-centered service, she has spent considerable time studying theories of human development in an effort to better understand individuals in the library's community.

What Could/Would Happen If . . .

. . . each of these librarians approach the following clients in the library. What developmental perspective(s) are in play? What service(s) would each be likely to provide? What level of effectiveness would be achieved?

- An eight-year-old boy who is having trouble with "story problems" in arithmetic

- A newly divorced man who is seeking custody of his daughter
- A woman who has just been promoted to the position of Vice President of South American Markets for her firm and is seeking to improve her Spanish
- An engaged couple who wish to hyphenate their combined names and are wondering what to do about a last name for any children that they may have
- A four-year-old who is afraid to participate in story hour
- A high school student with a paper due on AIDS
- A former actor who needs a script to prepare for a community theater audition
- A candidate for city council who wishes to find out about library needs
- A retired salesperson who lacks the money to travel and fears the thought of dying
- A college student with a learning disability
- An elementary teacher who wants a search done on computer graphics
- A young mother who has just learned that she has an incurable illness and is searching for information on the disease

NOTES

1. James C. Hansen, Richard R. Stevic, and Richard W. Warner, Jr., *Counseling: Theory and Process*, 2d ed. (Boston: Allyn & Bacon, 1977), 115-117.

2. Ibid., 126-127.

3. Ellie D. Evans and Boyd R. McCandless, *Children and Youth: Psychosocial Development*, 2d ed. (New York: Holt, Rinehart & Winston, 1978), 495-525.

4. Ibid., 277.

5. Erik Erikson, *Childhood and Society* (New York: W. W. Norton, 1963).

6. Russell D. Robinson, *An Introduction to Helping Adults Learn and Change* (Milwaukee: Bible Study Press, 1979), 16-21.

7. Malcolm S. Knowles, *The Modern Practice of Adult Education: From Pedagogy to Andragogy*, rev. ed. (Chicago: Association Press/Follett, 1980).

8. Margaret E. Monroe, "A Conceptual Framework for the Public Library as a Community Learning Center for Independent Study," *Library Quarterly* 46:1 (January 1976), 54-61.

9. Jonathan Kozol, *Illiterate America* (Garden City, NY: Anchor Press/Doubleday, 1985), 5.

10. Ibid., 57-58.

11. "Report of the National Commission on Excellence in Education" (Washington, DC: U.S. Government Printing Office, April 26, 1983).

12. A. J. Cropley, *Lifelong Education: A Psychological Analysis* (New York: Pergamon Press, 1977), 12.

Organizing for Effective Operations

Once the library's mission has been developed into a working philosophy of service . . . and the planning process is firmly in place as a routine and continuing blueprint for decision-making . . . and the client has been positioned as the appropriate vortex for all planning and implementation activities—it is then that the operational functions of management come into serious focus.

It is at this point that the library manager can effectively begin the function of organizing. Organizing involves:

- Determining the specific activities necessary to accomplish the planned goals

- Grouping the activities into a logical structure

- Assigning these activities to specific positions and people

- Providing a means for coordinating the efforts of individuals and groups[1]

These are formidable challenges to the manager and involve a range of components that will be discussed later in this chapter. However, those components plug into a more comprehensive pattern of management that acts as support and foundation for daily operations. This management sphere includes operating in the political arena, developing an appropriate range of policies, nurturing an effective library board, and creating partnerships with other libraries and agencies. This larger pattern will serve as a framework for subsequent discussion of organizational structures and activities.

THE POLITICAL ARENA

The essence of politics is the division of resources: The more limited the available resources, the more "political" the manager must become. Success in financial management of public agencies is closely tied to political success in obtaining the desired levels of program funding. Getting an adequate share of the limited resources available for appropriation by governing bodies is not an abstract consideration for program managers, and most financial decisions will depend on the level of funding provided.[2]

The library manager is the "orchestrator" of strategies in the political arena. Strategic possibilities are everywhere. For example, if the library is to receive an adequate funding base from which to operate, it is imperative that all library staff become proactive and involved in the life of the community. Such involvement includes being accountable in terms of identifying and responding to community needs, participating on community committees and boards, positioning the library as the information resource for community decision-making, and creating a climate where mutual benefit between the library and its clients is both present and acknowledged.

Library managers who suffer from a lack of political awareness and savvy may regard political efforts and analysis of the community as a frivolous use of staff time. Once the data are collected in conjunction with the planning process, such managers may file the results away without realizing the potential that such data represent for influencing political and decision-making processes. This power must be tapped in the future for the library to maintain parity with other community institutions.

POLICIES: EXTERNAL AND INTERNAL

Webster's New Twentieth Century Dictionary[3] defines policy as "any governing principle, plan, or course of action" and as "political wisdom or cunning; diplomacy; prudence; artfulness." Although the first definition may be more often preferred in the context of organizational management, it is interesting to note that the second definition listed is Webster's primary definition. The concept of policy may, therefore, be carried one step further. A policy is an objective or governing plan, but policy effectiveness is enhanced by the subjective qualities of political wisdom, cunning, and diplomacy.

This enhancement of policy implementation, although frequently overlooked, can be a critical factor in library operations. A policy, once established, is simply words on paper until it is activated; the subjective elements mentioned above create the climate in which the policy may flourish and serve as a tool of organization.

Attributes of Effective Policies

Policies are guidelines that lend direction to planning and decision-making. The functions of management are inefficient if performed in a vacuum without overall organization and direction. In addition, library services are at risk both theoretically and in practice if the underpinning of library policy is not in place to give needed support.

Policies are stated in broad terms, facilitating flexibility within a realistic structure. If a policy is written in too specific terms, the changing political, social, and economic climate will necessitate frequent revision. As the world's rate of change accelerates, flexibility of thought and action becomes increasingly critical to effective operation.

Policies anticipate a lengthy time line; they are written in terms of current and projected conditions. It would be an inefficient use of time and effort to create policies that are likely to be practical for only a limited period of time; in fact, such statements would be unlikely to fit the definition and intent of the policy in a variety of ways. The thoughtful preparation of policy language must move beyond the present and take into consideration the possibilities and trends of tomorrow.

Policies encourage equity and consistency in library operations. If policies are not in place to lend direction to decision-making at all levels of management, similar situations may produce disparate responses. No area of library operations would be unaffected—from the selection of materials to the hiring and termination of personnel. The resultant inconsistency and inequity would have serious ramifications in terms of staff morale and consumer relations. Policies promote clarity and justice in governance.

Policies are official statements of authority, having been developed, passed by formal motion, and recorded by the board of trustees. The importance of single-source authoritative direction cannot be stressed too strongly. If official statements were to be issued from a variety of sources within an organization, there would be a distinct likelihood that divergent opinions and positions would be expressed—resulting in confusion and chaos and certainly detracting from united movement toward goals. The formalization of procedures for policy creation and adoption provides the necessary stamp of credibility and identifies the parameters of jurisdiction.

Policies are purposefully made available to the public, the library board, and library staff so that all parties communicate from a common base of understanding. This aspect of policy implementation is vital to a library's marketing effort. Unless all constituencies are fully cognizant of what the library is about, misunderstandings and erroneous expectations are apt to occur. In addition, positive exposure to the library's perception of its mission and role in serving the community can facilitate the communication process.

Policies clarify, simplify, promote, and protect; they form the implementation core of the management system. Furthermore, the interactive nature of effective policy use enables modification of existing policies when such modification is desirable.

Appropriate policies can prevent potential problems from developing, protecting the library from unrealistic demands. In addition, policies serve as the foundation for the library's mission, supporting the entire planning process with statements of official purpose and direction.

Policies relate both to relationships external to library operations and to internal management organization and issues; differentiation between the two perspectives can be useful.

External Policies

There are basically three categories of external policies to consider: client-related, community-related, and intergovernmental-related.[4]

Client-related policies. Policies that relate directly to the library's clients include the hours of operation, eligibility requirements for use of the library, materials selection policies, circulation specifics, implementation of the new copyright law, and policies that provide guidelines for each program and service.

For example, selection policies usually cover responsibility for selection, scope, quality, and emphasis of the collection—including priorities; conditions for acceptance of gifts; relationship to local school curricula; and criteria for withdrawal of materials—including a grievance procedure for the handling of challenged materials. The "Library Bill of Rights" and "Freedom to Read Statement" of the American Library Association are usually included as well.

The importance of establishing these detailed policies cannot be overemphasized. In today's world of controversial issues and ideas, clear guidelines must be in place to defend library principles in the face of opposition and shifting community values.

Community-related policies. Policies concerned with the community are directed to such issues as the scope, hours, eligibility, and location of service, as well as guidelines for use of library facilities for nonlibrary functions. Patterns of both traditional and extratraditional library usage need to be articulated in order to assure equity and consistency to all persons in the community. Library facilities have value for community events that are quite apart from in-house library services. Frequently, such events serve as an outreach effort, encouraging citizens to enjoy the library in a more conventional mode once the initial unfamiliarity has been bridged. The public relations aspect of liberal policies regarding community use can be a definite asset as economic constraints tighten.

Intergovernmental-related policies. Linkages and relationships with other libraries and library systems through networking also need to be addressed by written policies. Elements to be considered include areas and limits of cooperation, the identity of cooperating agencies, and the interface with existing or potential state or regional networking plans. In addition, relationships with educational, other informational, human service, and political agencies should be delineated, with special attention paid to the methods and timing of joint planning efforts.

Marketing policies. A fourth category of external policy may be added to those already defined: the concepts and strategies of marketing within the overall planning process. The policies that govern the philosophy, scope, personnel, board responsibilities, and planning sequence of the marketing effort can provide the support structure necessary for continuous and effective marketing activities.

Internal Policies

In addition to the policies that delineate the relationships between the library and its various publics, policies are also necessary to guide internal library management and operations. The general categories include:

Overall operations. Policies in this area cover the authority and responsibility lines of the management structure. Personnel policies, supervisory functions, and organizational description are necessary components.

Library board operations. Procedures, rules, elections, legal liabilities, risk management, and general organization are delineated in sufficient detail so that the relationships among trustees and between the board and library staff and volunteers are clarified and articulated.

Budgets and financial management. Guidelines for funding, investments, and fiscal controls are established in order to facilitate efficient methods.

Property management. The responsibility of the board and library staff regarding physical assets, purchases, building programs, personal property, and insurance is defined.

Library policies, whether external or internal, are the core of the library's personality. Only the governing authority can make policy; this authority may or may not be the board of trustees, depending upon the legal nature of that board and whether its powers are advisory or carry legal responsibility. Together with the selection of the library director, the considered and creative establishment of effective library policies offers challenge and opportunity in this time of rapid change. The use of political wisdom in implementing those policies can make the difference between a static or dynamic library environment.

THE LIBRARY BOARD

Library policies are a thread woven through the cloth of library operations; they provide special strength, giving substance to the fabric of daily activities. Yet that thread could unravel if it were not secured at both ends. Ends could be secured by being fixed in knots, limiting flexibility and movement; conversely, each end could be held in place—by the library staff on one end and the library board on the other—with a positive tension, so that the thread supports yet is able to move freely to adapt to sudden stresses. This adaptive tensile strength between the library staff/administration and the library board has significant implications for effective library management.

Trustee Qualifications

Whether a library trustee belongs to a board with legal responsibilities or to a board with advisory powers only, there are certain qualifications closely related to competence and effectiveness:

- Sincere interest in the library's present and future.

- Knowledge of the community's social and economic conditions and trends, power structures, agencies and institutions, and demographics.

- Recognition and promotion of the library as the community's center of information transfer with significant educational, cultural, and recreational capabilities, responsibilities, and resources.

- Concern for sound management: systematic planning, accountability, staff development, creative policy formation, and innovative approaches.

- Perception of the clients' needs as primary and a willingness to establish cooperative relationships with other informational, educational, cultural, and recreational agencies in order to avoid needless duplication of services and resources.

- Ability to work well with others: board members, library staff, community leaders, and present and potential clients.

- Courage to sustain principles of intellectual freedom and to withstand pressures that would erode these principles; adherence to due process of law.

- An open and curious approach to life, with respect for other points of view.

- Readiness to devote time, talent, and effort in the pursuit of trustee duties and library concerns.

Ideally, every appointed or elected trustee would possess all of these traits. In practical terms, however, ideals are really goals, which must be articulated, internalized, and continually pursued. Therefore, although this list of qualifications may seem to be necessary a priori, in practical terms successful attainment of these characteristics requires a mutual effort by trustee and librarian—for it is the librarian who acts as guide, educator, and mentor in the process.

The beginnings of this mentoring relationship can be found in the orientation program, which the librarian initiates by inviting the new trustee and the board president/chairperson to a welcoming session in the library. During this session, questions and answers are exchanged, and copies of the library's policies, goals and objectives, and recent minutes are provided for the new board member. In addition, discussion may include philosophy of library service, mutual expectations, development and organization of the library, and opportunities for trustee involvement at local, state, and national levels. Frequently, a tour of the library is provided, with introductions to available staff members.

Continuing orientation occurs through the appointment of the new trustee to one or more board committees. This experience encourages in-depth participation and close interaction with other board members. Additional strategies for continuing education include encouraging attendance at conferences (paid if possible), distribution of one or more recent articles from library journals prior to each board meeting (attached to the agenda), and agenda time for discussion of the articles and other issues of interest.

Duties and Responsibilities

The library board enjoys the public trust. Duties and responsibilities inherent in this public trust may be loosely classified as being of two kinds: the legal responsibilities specifically enjoined upon the board by statute, and the practical responsibilities related to daily operation of the library.[5] Because the first category, statutory board powers, differs from state to state, all that is mentioned here is the existence of such legal authority. The reader is directed to seek out the specific tenets of local state statutes that are pertinent and appropriate.

The practical responsibilities, however, can be placed in generalized categories that apply across local situations and are primarily concerned with the relationship between the library board and the library staff. A simple rule of thumb can be stated succinctly: The library board hires the library director, adopts policies, and performs other duties as required by law; the library staff operates the library. This is a critical distinction, and the line between policy and operations should not be crossed; when that happens, the consequent blurring of roles causes considerable anxiety and stress.

Briefly, some of the other trustee duties may include: determining the library's mission, securing adequate funds, knowing the community, working with the staff in a planning process, working with the budget, knowing local and state laws, attending all board meetings, attending professional meetings, working with the state library agency, and reporting to the public in accountable terms. In sum, the library board must play a policy role and a supportive role in order to enable the library staff to create an effective information environment for the community. However, this environment also requires ongoing cooperation and behavior protocol.

Cooperation and Protocol

Cooperation between library board members and staff is the functional linkage that allows a close working relationship. A basic structure for effective cooperation is the recognition of protocol. For example, disagreement among board members should be discussed openly in the board meeting, but all members of the board should accede to the decision of the majority when policy matters are voted upon. Independent judgment and action exceed the authority of any individual board member once that vote is taken.

In addition, supplementary information and advice need to be supplied by the library director. Because the director is in daily contact with both library operations and the public, he or she is in the strongest position to make recommendations to the library board. Mutual trust is of paramount importance. The library director needs the secure knowledge that the library board will support administrative efforts to carry out existing policies; conversely, the library board must be confident that the library administration will conscientiously implement those policies.

Another aspect of protocol is the adherence to organizational design. There is a definite structure that facilitates appropriate behavior: The library director is hired by and continues to report to the library board; library staff members are officially hired by and report to the library director or designate. Although each library has its own organizational structure with various patterns of management and responsibility, the ultimate authority for personnel decisions rests with the director (not to be confused with personnel policy, which is the responsibility of the library board).

Responsibility to the Profession

Professional growth is everyone's responsibility, particularly in an era of unprecedented change. Though it may not be a primary responsibility, the board does have a unique and influential contribution to make in promoting continuing education opportunities among staff—both philosophically and with appropriate monetary and work-release incentives. Continuing education can and should be viewed as an investment in the library's present and future growth, as well as a demonstration of trust and confidence in the profession of library and information studies. It is the library administration's province to arrange work scheduling and budgetary language to accommodate staff development; the library board's responsibility is to provide supportive policies and budgetary authority for such endeavors. In addition, board members can consult with state library agency personnel to explore possible sources of grants, scholarships, or other funding for continuing education purposes. If the library is a member of a library system, this may be the channel through which state and/or federal monies are distributed.

It should not be overlooked that library board members are also subject to the winds of change and can benefit themselves from participation in continuing education opportunities. Noncredit courses designed and promoted for the library community—and occasionally for trustees specifically—may be offered by various providers of continuing education, including universities, state library agencies, library systems, and professional associations.

A particularly valuable expression of trustee interest can come through active involvement in professional associations at local, state, and national levels. For example, the American Library Association and its chapters usually include a subsidiary group designed for library trustees. The rewards of membership to the individual trustee, the library, and the profession at large are significant and far outweigh the expenditure of time and money involved.

Some of the services provided by professional associations include programs, publications, and workshops. Services offered by trustee divisions are designed to help trustees make the connection between local library operations and the opportunities and problems of libraries in general. Topics addressed may include trustee responsibility, legislative concerns, lobbying, budgeting and funding, and intellectual freedom, as well as current issues in the field. In addition, the networking aspect of association membership is an important consideration. Both interpersonal networking and the group efforts that can be organized to influence library legislation are vital results of in-depth participation in professional associations. Trustees can and should view themselves as critical elements in overall library effectiveness.

Mutual trust is basic to trustee responsibility: trust among members of the library board; trust between the board and the administration; trust among trustees and library staff; and trust in the movement toward maximum service through cooperation among system members. The role of the library trustee is complex, yet it can be stimulated by a sense of dedication to the premise that the public library has the potential to be a vital force in the information society.

PARTNERSHIPS WITH OTHER LIBRARIES AND AGENCIES

In order to explore the potential role of the library as a partner with other libraries and agencies, we must leave behind the traditional and limited view of the library as a physical structure that houses and protects information for the scholar. The public library that is to be an integral part—ideally, the nerve center—of the community must be willing and able to move and grow with local needs—and cooperate with other organizations who also seek to meet those needs.

Partnership implies a voluntary joining of effort with the expectation of some type of gain or reward. It is not a defensive collaboration predicated on the alleviation or avoidance of a negative situation. Rather, partnership is goal-oriented, and founded on a perceived benefit.

A proactive posture is necessary in effective partnership. The dynamism required for a truly proactive and assertive approach is the catalyst that offers the greatest probability of success. Partnership thrives in this electric environment, providing the climate for a continuous nurturing cycle. It is vital that partners view both the requisite amount of effort and the ensuing rewards as equitable to both parties. This sense of fairness maintains an equilibrium and desirable tension in the relationship, keeping friction and stress to a minimum.

These perspectives on partnership can be applied whether the union is between corporate bodies, individuals, agencies, or organizations. The necessary elements are melded by the communication process, which undergirds, spans, and links them together. Communication can inject either lubricant or grit into the working of a partnership. Keeping the system operating smoothly in all directions is a fundamental requirement if the partnership is to succeed.

A Roadmap to Partnership

Pragmatic cooperative ventures grow from the roots of philosophical unity and acceptance of shared purpose. Theory and practice form a genuine amalgam in partnerships that work. Where mission is held in common, implementation of successful activities is a reasonable result. Therefore, discussion of organizational goals is necessary before specific plans are generated. Once areas of mutual purpose are identified, the following sequence can be used to map strategy—within, of course, the structure of each partner's formal planning process.

Impact objectives. Both partners need to acknowledge and recognize that impact will be greater because of the coordinated thrust than it would have been within the purview of a single agency. If one planning "eye" is kept on the desired impact and if objectives are developed with that result in mind, the entire process will have more direction and a stronger probability of successful completion.

Situational analysis. As in the discussion of the library as broker, a community analysis is a logical point of departure. Elements to be specifically considered within the context of partnership are

- The definition of the "problem," or focus area, as perceived from the several viewpoints of the cooperating agencies. These disparate views can give a three-dimensional character to the focus area that a single agency is unlikely to discern; it is one of the early advantages of cooperative activity.

- The time factor. This "best guess" estimate of the time required for resolution of the problem can be effectively designed on a continuum, ranging from minimum allotment (often influenced by monetary or political constraint) to desired maximum length. Contingency plans (alternatives) can be devised to intersect at several points on this time continuum.

- The arena for activity. This factor may be defined geographically (based on physical or political boundaries), stratified in terms of target market, or governed by the nature or interests of the agency partners. These parameters delimit the extent of activity and are important to have in place before concrete action plans are created.

- Possible additional partners. Although the original partners have initiated the project, it may become gradually apparent that certain other agencies may have interests or goals that could enhance the activity. If so, it may be of mutual advantage to increase the number of partners in the venture.

It is critical that a genuine philosophical and resource commitment be given by each partner; ideally, the cooperative activity will be at approximately the same level in each agency's individual organizational priorities. Without active commitment and a mutual consensus to undertake the activity, the notion of equality is abridged and one of the foundations of partnership is dangerously compromised.

Negotiation. Once the above steps are firmly in place, the planning process can move rapidly forward. Goals, objectives, and action plans are negotiated until procedural consensus is achieved. With one eye on the impact objectives and the other on individual agency interests and concerns, the building of the plan is a relatively routine exercise.

These steps in partnership are admittedly complex: multiple points of view can raise hidden perspectives on a problem, but they also can generate multiple possible solutions. The complexity becomes unwieldy only if the positive tension in the partnership is not carefully tended: Equal effort for equal reward is the working formula.

There are a variety of possible partners for the public library. The following comments will focus first on partnership with other libraries through membership in a library system, then on cooperation with various agencies through information and referral, and finally on joint ventures with educational institutions.

Target: The Library System

There is a growing level of cooperation between individual libraries and public and/or intertype library systems. A variety of support mechanisms are provided by library systems: access to additional materials through interloan, consultant expertise, technical advice, and access to state and/or federal monies. Each member library can draw upon system resources to help meet local needs.

It is important, however, that potential expansion of services and resources be weighed carefully against perceived loss of autonomy. In most communities, careful investigation by the library board of the possibilities inherent in system membership usually puts to rest preconceived fears and apprehension. Although contractual and legal arrangements must be worked through—as in any business relationship—the forfeiture of local identity tends to diminish as a major concern. The recognition of the library system as a major force in strengthening library service among all member libraries soon overcomes hesitation.

As the costs of materials and services escalate, the advantages of cooperative efforts through system membership become more readily apparent. In a less pragmatic and more visionary sense, the opportunities presented by system membership enable local libraries to become more completely that window to the world that is the ultimate goal of library service.

Target: The Library as Broker

What is more natural—at least in idealistic terms—than the image of the public library serving as the nerve center of the community, the point of first recourse when a citizen needs information, assistance, or opportunity for learning? If the public library is indeed to become the nerve center of the community, a variety of factors must enter into its design. The planning process is a first structural step; once this process is firmly in place, implementation functions can begin.

At this point in the discussion, the assumption is made that this ideal public library has determined that its mission includes the clearinghouse function and that this service will be the linkage between the community's citizens, in-house provision of information, and referral to other community sources.

It logically follows that the library's clients encompass the totality of the community, the entire spectrum of individuals and groups; yet this is not entirely the case. Although the library needs to "be there" for all citizens, good management dictates that planning focus be directed to specific target markets. These targeted clients may change from planning year to planning year in line with community change and client response; the library can no longer afford the philosophical luxury of "being all things to all people," and specific managerial targets must be set. Market segmentation philosophy suggests that target groups be identified for concentrated service and that other groups receive less attention. Although it may seem harsh, this approach does recognize the realities of library service and today's fiscal pressures.

As patterns of inequality of access are identified, however, the library staff can engage in outreach activities to extend library service beyond present configurations and target new or different markets. Outreach has evolved to mean deliberate planned attempts to make significant contact with specific community groups who have a record of little or no interaction with the library. These attempts have usually involved new structures of service, new or expanded collections in target areas, new or revised delivery systems, and, most important, new attitudes on the part of staff. The importance of staff attitude is emphasized because the outreach effort has little chance of success without commitment—it eats up time, energy, enthusiasm, and imagination at a rapid rate. But outreach is so vital to the library's overall relationship with its community that the effort is well worth the expenditure of human energy.

However, the brokering effort is one service that can truly "be there" as an access point for any and all clients. The simple existence of such a service, coupled with the desire to be central to community activity, will not, of course, achieve this goal; effective marketing strategies will also be required.

One marketing strategy of particular value to the establishment of a brokering role is the marketing audit (see chapter 2). Through analysis of the community, the following questions can be addressed:

- What is the community? How can it be defined geographically, demographically, politically, psychographically, and so forth?

- What resources are already available in the library? What information can be secured from other agencies and groups? Who are the contact persons?

- What can be learned through formal methods, such as surveys or interviews? Can informal observation be useful? Such observation is frequently accomplished by library personnel actually walking the streets of the community. This strategy has added significance in that the data collected are only one benefit; a secondary benefit is the exposure that library staff secure for the library in the process of meeting and greeting citizens. The library demonstrates its concern and caring about the needs of its constituency and information transfer flows in both directions: citizens to staff and staff to citizens. An added plus is that interaction occurs with a cross-section of citizens, not just library users.

This extensive collection of information about the community not only provides the library with the data it needs to deliver comprehensive service—it also creates a database that can be used by the library/clearinghouse to make accurate and effective referrals to external resources. If, indeed, the goal is to promote the library as the first place to contact in regard to an information or education need, it is imperative that rapid and correct response be given to each query.

There is also a natural relationship between the understanding of human needs and development (chapter 3) and the serving of clients in the public library. Expanding the scope of the reference interview into an information and referral program enhances the role of the library as broker to the community, helping clients with coping strategies. Coping is difficult, for anyone and everyone. Various institutions have achieved varying degrees of success in helping people deal with personal and environmental crises. Churches, schools, and social service agencies are but a few of the many institutions in which this helping function is at least part of the mission.

The problem that inevitably arises, however, is one of scope. Each of these institutions is admirably equipped to successfully assist with a discrete problem area. No agency or institution has had either the expertise or the latitude to address the diversity present in the three-dimensional, whole human being. This problem is to be expected, as each institution has a defined focus to its activities.

But the public library can be different; it stands ready to serve its clientele on the entire front of human experience. Further, there are no restrictions of age, educational level, income, race, religious affiliation, and so forth to limit who is served. In other words, the public library is an omnibus institution that can legitimately address these human problems and aid clients in developing the requisite coping strategies—serving as broker, as switching point, as referral point to the specific help that will meet each need.

In today's information-overloaded society, people are apt to be dazzled by both the volume of data and the available technology. It is certainly easier to ask for the trusted opinion of a relative or friend— regardless of the reliability and accuracy of that information—than to try and puzzle out where other sources of answers might be found. It is this confusion that forms the void into which the public library must step if it is to be a meaningful component of community life. Filling this void can mean survival to the library as an institutional entity and to the citizen as a coping agent in the midst of change.

The public library is a unique institution in its traditions of neutrality and access. There is no institution better suited—by either historical development or inherent mission—to serve the clearinghouse role. But if the public library is to be the initial contact point for location of information and referral to other sources, librarians need to create a network of contacts with persons in each of these corollary agencies. In this way, information can be readily updated, and a known individual can be the referral contact in each agency. In addition, mutual sharing of information, concerns, and problems is facilitated through personal interaction with professionals in these several agencies.

Target: Educational Institutions

The public library can work cooperatively with public and private schools to expand the scope of opportunity available to self-directed students, both formally and informally. As a supplement to the classroom and the instructional materials center, the public library has the capacity to add a depth of resources that may be difficult to achieve in a school situation. The public librarian can attend faculty meetings to ascertain curricular needs and use the latitude of the library's collection to augment the school's capability. The benefits of interlibrary loan can be called upon when needed. This level of collaboration requires good communication and a positive working relationship among librarians, teachers, and both school and library administrations.

Cooperation need not be limited to K-12; the public library can serve as campus library for noncampus higher education (such as universities without walls and extended degree programs) and supplement libraries of two-year (or even four-year) colleges as the situation indicates. The possibilities are varied and challenging.

From another point of view, it is tremendously valuable to library staff (particularly in libraries with a designated departmental structure) to maintain close professional ties with local academic departments. The public librarian's educational credentials and expertise in subject areas must be maintained at the highest possible level of currency. It is entirely appropriate—and beneficial to both—for librarians and professors to forge strong academic links and share expertise. The credibility of the public librarian as a legitimate subject specialist can be greatly enhanced by concrete connections with the academic community. Too often, the professional image of the public librarian is diminished by citizen perceptions (i.e., that librarian activity centers around checking out books and reading all the new fiction). If professionalism is to be recognized, the public's perception of the librarian must be grounded in that individual's subject-oriented expertise. The acknowledged expertise of the library professional should be emphasized in the library's marketing efforts.

As in all partnerships, the ingredient of equity in the educational relationship is readily apparent. There is much to be gained by the educational institutions, the professional scholars and librarians, and the clients—the students. The quest for knowledge is an exciting and challenging pursuit. It requires a combined effort to chip away at the burgeoning volume of information that threatens to bury the intellectually curious. By working together, public libraries and other educational institutions can increase student access to the intricacies of information retrieval and smooth the pathway to learning. It can be one of the most rewarding of partnerships.

In summary, it must be emphatically restated that the concept of cooperation and the proactive posture of partnership are imperatives in order for present and future public library service to achieve maximum strength and effectiveness. In addition, the power of networking must never be undervalued or underestimated. The strength of the ties among professionals facing similar problems and situations can visibly increase the effectiveness of the service provided to clients. The negative sense of operating in a vacuum or in isolation is diminished, if not eliminated. Networking forges channels of communication, creates bonds where none may have existed, and multiplies individual capabilities manyfold. The advantages of cooperative effort toward a common goal far exceed the work required by each individual and/or agency to achieve such cooperation. This is organization on a macro level and can be immensely helpful to the manager in organizing on the micro, or library, level.

ORGANIZATIONAL STRUCTURES AND CLIMATE

The manager is impacted at the library level by the norms and practices of the organizational climate and a personal set of values and beliefs. In the larger environment discussed above, both organization and manager must interact with other organizations and managers who are influenced by similar forces. Therefore, the library manager must walk a tightrope that is continually swayed by self-interest (on the part of oneself and others), change at a variety of levels, and events that may or may not be controllable.

Response to these internal and external forces can vary but typically will fall into (and/or between) one of two cycles: bureaucratic and entrepreneurial. Each cycle has four parts:

Bureaucratic
1. The *Patriarchal Contract* assumes a top-down, high-control organizational structure

2. *Myopic Self-interest*, concern with personal rewards and moving up the hierarchy

3. *Manipulative Tactics*, behavior that is strategic, cautious, and indirect (often a traditional definition of "political")

4. *Dependency*, the belief that survival is in someone else's control

Entrepreneurial
1. The *Entrepreneurial Contract* is based on the belief that the most trustworthy source of authority comes from within

2. *Enlightened Self-interest*, a definition of success in terms of contribution and service to clients; rewards are seen as jobs with meaning, the opportunity to learn and create, the chance to grow

3. *Authentic Tactics*, in terms of sharing information and control, taking reasonable risks, and acting directly based on personal values

4. *Autonomy*, the seeking of which reduces the need to give attention and power to those higher up in the organization[6]

These two cycles might be viewed as two poles of a continuum, but in the real world they illustrate two discrete approaches toward managing in general and organizing in particular. The bureaucratic model was developed in the industrial sector and has been effective in managing organizations with very well-defined levels of staffing and reporting within the framework of a top-down hierarchy. However, today's world requires an organizational structure that is more entrepreneurial in design, a structure that can adapt more easily and quickly to a changing environment. Therefore, it is the second cycle that is to be preferred if the library's management seeks to be in tune with the community's needs and climate.

Another way to view these two approaches might be termed "results-oriented" and "people-oriented." However, this perspective would be shortsighted, as the entrepreneurial model readily seeks to maximize both results and people—much as the maxim cited in *The One Minute Manager* that states, "People Who Feel Good About Themselves Produce Good Results."[7]

Peter Drucker has addressed this point by stating that "the purpose of an organization is to enable common men to do uncommon things" and that organizations exist "to make ordinary human beings perform better than they seem capable of, to bring out whatever strength there is in its members, and to use each man's strength to help all the other members perform."[8]

Therefore, the overriding goal for effective organizing is to develop a structure and an administrative attitude that approximates the entrepreneurial style as closely as is reasonable, taking into consideration the range of variables that are unique to each library's situation. Just as the planning process was proposed as a more appropriate approach than arbitrary standards because no two communities are exactly alike, so, too, the organizational structure that will best serve a given library will depend upon the human and political variables particular to that library and its environment.

Based upon the data gleaned from the marketing audit—data that have been organized into patterns of information and subsequently synthesized into knowledge areas producing goals and objectives—the library manager is now ready to develop an organizational structure that will prove to be both effective and efficient. In this effort, the manager and staff, together with the planning team, work to create this structure by:

- Determining the specific activities necessary to accomplish the planned goals.

- Grouping those activities into a logical structure.

- Assigning the selected activities to specific positions and people.

- Providing a means for coordinating the efforts of both individuals and groups.[9]

The structure that emerges may have any one of a myriad of configurations and will more closely resemble one or more points on a series of many continuum models than any static polar extremes. What are some possibilities? The following list illustrates this multiplicity of continuum options:

Holistic operations . . . . . departmentalization

Single outlet . . . . . multiple outlets

Specialized products . . . . . generalized products

Vertical hierarchy . . . . . more participatory models[10]

Centralized . . . . . decentralized authority

Line positions . . . . . staff positions

It is helpful for both staff and community if the structure that emerges is illustrated in graphic terms through an organizational chart (see figs. 4.1 to 4.4). However, regardless of the type of structure, the successful library operation will, as emphasized in other chapters, focus on the client and develop appropriate products to meet identified client needs.

Change is a situational reality that presents a constant challenge to library management. The library manager who seeks to create an organizational structure that is both adaptable and flexible, capable of operating proactively in a community in which the societal and technological contexts change continually, must employ certain strategies that will nurture this organic capability:

- Multidirectional communication flow

- Flexibility rather than rigidity in terms of policies, procedures, job descriptions, and so forth

- An emphasis on authority rooted in expertise rather than position power

- An ongoing redefinition of staffing and operations that recognizes a networking rather than an institutional perspective

- A commitment to the concept of the library as a local node in a global information system

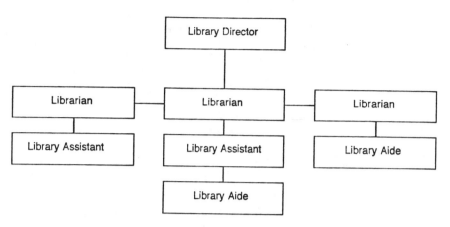

Fig. 4.1. A Hierarchical Organizational Chart.

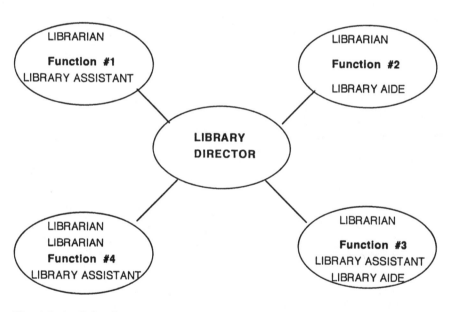

Fig. 4.2. An Orbit Organizational Structure. Each function has a lead worker; leadership changes at appropriate intervals.

	Librarian 1	Librarian 2	Librarian 3
Function 1	**X**	X	X
Function 2	X	**X**	X
Function 3	X	X	**X**

Fig. 4.3. Matrix Organizational Chart. Large "X" indicates leadership role; each librarian serves in leadership or membership capacities for each function.

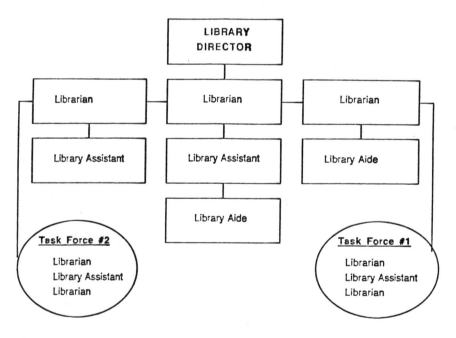

Fig. 4.4. A Task Force Approach to Organization.

The public library is in a unique position to serve both as focal point for the community's information needs and as window to the world of information. This position can be nurtured through its organizational structure and attitudes. Within an effective structure, members of the staff can be empowered to use their talents in significant ways. Chapter 5 will focus on personnel and staffing issues and opportunities—the roots and substance of a properly tilled organizational garden.

For Discussion

- How well does your library staff operate in the political environment? How could this situation improve?
- What policies are presently in place in your library?
- What is the relationship between your library board and your library administration? between the board and the staff?
- How professionally committed and involved are the members of your library's staff?
- What partnerships with other libraries and agencies in your community are presently in place? What partnerships are possible?
- Is your library a member of a library system? What are the benefits? the limitations?
- On a scale of 1 to 5, how close is your library to being the brokering "nerve center" of your community?
  1_____2_____3_____4_____5
  Not at all   Very close
- What cooperative ventures are in place with local educational institutions?
- Describe the organizational climate in your library.

Scenario Four
Who Is Really in Charge?

The Facts

Delta Public Library is located in a suburban community just outside a major metropolitan area.

A group of concerned parents has demanded that the Delta Public Library remove a list of 14 titles from its collection.

The list includes books, videos, and audiocassettes.

The allegation has been made that these titles are inappropriate for circulation to anyone under the age of 18.

What Could/Would Happen If . . .

- No selection policy and procedures for challenged materials have been established.
- A selection policy has been recently put into effect, but the language of the policy consistently refers to "books."
- The library director has been the author of a weekly column in the local newspaper for three years. Many of the columns have dealt with intellectual freedom issues and the library's selection and circulation policies.
- Two members of the library board are among the concerned parents who presented the demand.
- Two members of the city council are among the concerned parents who presented the demand.
- The library board favors "micromanaging" library operations.
- The library board and the director have worked out a clear division of responsibilities, with the board responsible for making policy decisions and the director charged with implementation.
- The members of the city council have great respect for the library director but feel an obligation to "monitor" how city funds are spent.
- The library operates with a management team, and communication among staff is at a very high level.
- The director is from the "old school," retaining all decision-making power; staff frequently skip over the "chain of command" and speak directly to library board or city council members. Although policies are "on the books," enforcement is spotty at best.

NOTES

1. Robert D. Stueart and Barbara B. Moran, *Library Management*, 3d ed. (Littleton, CO: Libraries Unlimited, 1987), 54.

2. Peter Hamon, Darlene E. Weingand, and Al Zimmerman, *Budgeting and the Political Process for Libraries: Simulation Games* (Littleton, CO: Libraries Unlimited, 1992).

3. *Webster's New Twentieth Century Dictionary*, unabridged, 2d ed. (Cleveland, OH: Collins/World, 1975).

4. Opinion Research Associates, Inc., *Wisconsin Library Trustee Reference Manual* (Madison, WI: Department of Public Instruction, 1980), Section I, 3-10.

5. Virginia G. Young, *The Library Trustee: A Practical Guidebook*, 4th ed. (Chicago: American Library Association, 1988), 9.

6. Peter Block, *The Empowered Manager: Positive Political Skills at Work* (San Francisco: Jossey-Bass, 1989), 20-24.

7. Kanneth Blanchard and Spencer Johnson, *The One Minute Manager* (New York: Berkley, 1982), 19.

8. Peter F. Drucker, *Management: Tasks, Responsibilities, Practices* (New York: Harper & Row, 1974), 455.

9. Stueart and Moran, *Library Management*, 54.

10. Such participatory models include matrix structure, orbit structure, and task force structure.

Staffing for Service

The well-tilled organizational ground has the capacity to provide nourishment and support for a variety of personnel functions and personalities. Putting such support to one side for a moment, it is important to recognize the economic imperative to develop an excellent staff; staff cost is typically the largest part of any public library budget, ranging from 60 to 80 percent. Accountability would suggest that prudent stewardship entails hiring and developing the library's human resources to the most effective level.

Carrying this argument one step further, it is not unreasonable to assert that the public library's relationship to its community is grounded in the efforts and attitudes of the library staff. A library may have an excellent collection and an award-winning building, but if the staff is not competent and client-centered, these material resources will not be effectual in meeting community needs. Therefore, understanding principles of personnel management and applying them in the context of good service to the library's clients are twin imperatives for the library manager.

PERSONNEL PRINCIPLES

Because the human resources of the library command the greater part of the library's budget, good personnel practice mandates that effective management principles be directed toward the interaction between managers and staff members. In this regard, the traditional and outdated view of the library as a storehouse of materials casts a long shadow over both present accountability and future promise. Until the true importance of staff to the information transaction is acknowledged—and demonstrated through adequate salaries and lines of authority—the library's role as broker to the world of information cannot be secured.

This fundamental perceptual change involves the relationship between the library and its publics, to be sure, but it must begin with the relationship between the library and its staff. Librarians have traditionally emerged from the humanities and the social sciences; only in recent years have the sciences added significantly to the mix.

Consequently, librarians have often entered the profession because they love books and ideas and have instinctively recoiled from the somewhat "shady" concepts of measurement, marketing, reward, and punishment.

Today, however, these "shady" practices from the profit sector are being reexamined, and bridges to nonprofit institutions are emerging. Phrases such as "product," "goals and objectives," "cost-effectiveness," and "zero-based budgeting" have crept into the literature, heralding a new look in library management.

Most of this new look begins at the level of upper management in the context of the "big picture," but ideas of this nature must flow through the entire organization if any movement toward organizational change is to realistically occur. The planning principles discussed in chapter 2 apply as significantly to internal operations as to external ones. Seeing that everyone affected by a decision is included in the decision-making process creates the "ownership" that is so critical to carrying decisions through. The complexity of people will be an eternal challenge, but the energy that is available can dramatically transform an organization.

Formal and Informal Organizational Patterns

Library staff members are part of an organization that operates in both formal and informal patterns. There are levels of activity that relate to functions to be performed; these levels may be organized in many different ways, ranging from more hierarchical to more decentralized. The formal organization of an institution addresses itself to two purposes: the economic purposes of the total enterprise and the securing of cooperative effort.[1]

Yet this is just one obvious dimension. There is more to social organization than surface structure. Many of the patterns of human interaction are quite separate from the face that the institution presents to the outside world; the organizational chart is like a photograph—and just as two-dimensional. In order to breathe life into an institution, the distinctions of social distance, movement, and equilibrium among and between individuals must be considered. Further, there is a hierarchy of prestige that differentiates between the work of one person vis-à-vis another.

In addition, there are sentiments and values residing in the social organization that informally differentiate, order, and integrate individuals and groups. Such informal social organizations exist in every institution and, in the ideal situation, actually facilitate the functioning of the formal organization. However, there are times when formal and informal structures develop in opposition; therefore, it is important to recognize these interrelationships and facilitate them toward pursuit of common ideas and beliefs (mission), goals, and objectives.[2]

Policies and Procedures

This facilitation is aided by the development of policies and procedures that both represent and nurture the library's mission, goals, and objectives. Chapter 4 covered the broad profile of library policies, but specific policies concerning personnel matters are more appropriately detailed here. The creation of formal policies provides the necessary framework for consistency in personnel practice. The following are important points to be included in a personnel policy:

Employment practices—affirmative action, equal opportunity, recruitment, selection, hiring, job and position descriptions; provision for probationary appointments, with length of time specified; provision for hiring substitute staff when needed. It is important that there is a description of each job in the library, with degree of responsibility, educational and other qualifications required, special abilities or skills required, and salary scale.

Personnel actions—probation, performance review, tenure, promotion, reassignment, demotion, suspension or other disciplinary action, reinstatement, records, in-service training, layoff, dismissal, resignation. Language should be included concerning termination of employment, whether voluntary or involuntary, including amount of notice required and a stipulation that resignations should be in writing; guidelines for coaching and disciplinary actions; and a statement concerning grievance procedures, appeals, and other protection against unfair discharge or demotion.

Salary administration—salary schedules, giving minimum and maximum salary or wages, amount of increments, period between increments, etc.; pay dates; deductions.

Employee benefits—a listing of Social Security and fringe benefits, coordinating (as appropriate) with those available to other public employees—i.e., health and hospitalization, life and income continuation insurance; pension plans; workers' compensation coverage; vacation and other leaves (paid or unpaid), including sick leave, holidays (list of legal holidays observed), and education benefits, including whether paid time and/or paid fees are provided; eligibility of part-time employees for benefits.

Work conditions—hours, scheduling, flexible time, job sharing, overtime, compensatory time; an outline of what constitutes a regular work week with specified number of hours; a statement concerning number and length of work breaks; a statement regarding attendance at library meetings—who attends, whether time off with pay and/or travel expenses are awarded; a statement concerning working conditions—adequate heat, light, rest rooms, etc.

These personnel policies may be unique to the library or may be tied to the requirements of the municipality. In any event, it is the responsibility of the library board to assure that such policy language is in effect.

Levels of Staffing

Most libraries hire employees at various levels of responsibility and educational background. Library managers and supervisory staff commonly hold the first professional degree, a master's degree in library and information studies (MLS). In larger libraries, line librarians are also likely to be MLS graduates. In addition, larger facilities may also employ specialists in computer science, public relations, and/or business administration. These professionals have the background and expertise to perform in leadership roles and are most effectively utilized in nonroutine tasks that require the knowledge and expertise that they have acquired.

Support staff form an important component of the personnel profile and may include library assistants, clerical personnel, and so on. This category typically has the largest number of persons employed by the library, and the duties performed include inputting, coding, and verifying bibliographic data; maintaining book funds; ordering; circulating materials; claiming serials; filing; and copy cataloging. Routine operations are usually the province of support staff, and the educational preparation for these positions varies widely, from a high school diploma to graduate degrees of various kinds.[3]

In smaller public libraries, where there are fewer positions (perhaps only one or two individuals, both in part-time employment), this spectrum of expertise and educational backgrounds may not exist. In the smallest situations, the notion of what is "professional" will not match the prevailing definition promulgated by library associations (i.e., a master's degree in a program accredited by the American Library Association). In these smaller towns, "professional" must rightly apply to dedication and attitude, regardless of educational preparation. This is not to discount the importance of the full master's degree; rather, it is an attempt to acknowledge both the reality of what a small community can afford and the hardworking, committed librarians who serve those communities.

It is a challenge to effectively match personnel with appropriate work under any circumstances, particularly in today's workplace, where professional growth and job satisfaction have become expectations. The counterpoint to these expectations occurs when economic conditions preclude the number—or even existence—of career ladders. When promotion based upon merit is not possible, it is incumbent upon library management to creatively seek out opportunities to provide alternative enriching experiences that will continue to motivate excellent staff members.

Motivation

All too often, the road to career enhancement is perceived as being possible only through upward mobility. In fact, most staff will view moving into management as a necessary step if salary and responsibility levels are to be increased. Ideally, there should be career progression options that reward excellence in public and technical services—perhaps several levels of reward tied to competence, performance, and mastery.

When an employee views a job as rewarding, there is a definite effect on his or her commitment to that job—resulting in yet more satisfaction on the part of the employee and very real benefits to the organization. Three methods of adding value to a job include the following:

1. *Assigning work that enables the employee to achieve personal goals.* For example, does the individual have special skills or abilities that are not being utilized in the current assignment? An employee with artistic abilities could be asked to assist in the design of exhibits, posters, or public relations materials. Employees who have developed strong writing skills could be assigned to some tasks that would utilize those abilities, such as writing a newsletter or preparing an annual report. In the case of employees who seek career advancement, the library manager can provide opportunities for growth by offering job enlargement, assignment to special projects, job sharing or exchange, and/or participation in staff development activities.

2. *Helping the employee achieve internal rewards, such as a sense of accomplishment and an increase in self-esteem.* For example, the manager can help the employee develop realistic and attainable goals and objectives so that achievements will be both possible and evident to the employee, the manager, and co-workers. Recognition through public praise by the manager, a formal letter of appreciation for the employee's personnel file, and inclusion in a staff achievement program are important ways to acknowledge achievement and increase the self-esteem of an individual employee.

3. *Reinforcing successful achievement on the part of the employee by providing external rewards such as promotions, merit salary increases, or a valued assignment.* For example, an appointment to a key problem-solving committee or task force may provide a strong reward for achievement. Membership in a group charged with solving a significant problem or implementing a major project can be both broadening and stimulating to the employee. Other possibilities include moving the employee to a better office (perhaps with a window), paying for tuition or conference expenses, or establishing a higher-level title.[4]

Frederick Herzberg made a significant contribution to motivational theory in the late 1950s when he surveyed 203 engineers and accountants in nine industrial sites in Pittsburgh.[5] He asked two questions relating to job satisfaction: 1) Think of a work-related incident that happened in your life that made you feel very negative about what happened and tell me why it made you feel negative; and 2) think of a work-related incident that happened in your life that made you feel good about what happened and tell me why it made you feel good. Based on the results of the responses, he determined that there was a cluster of five negative factors and five positive factors. Negative feelings were engendered by:

- Policy and administration
- Supervision
- Relationship with supervisor
- Work conditions
- Salary (presumably considered too low)

Positive feelings were generated by these five factors:

- Achievement
- Recognition
- The work itself
- Responsibility
- Advancement

It seems clear that organizational policy and administration are primary catalysts for negative reactions, and these environmental attributes can be viewed as correlating with the lower levels in Maslow's hierarchy of needs (see fig. 5.1): physical/survival needs and security/safety needs.[6] Therefore, the case can be made that these needs must be satisfied and the working environment must be considered adequate in order to allow upper-level needs to emerge.

Maslow's upper-level needs of social/belonging and esteem/ego fit nicely with the five factors generating positive feelings, culminating with the peak goal of self-actualization, or fulfillment of one's potential. Fundamentally rooted in internal motivation but nourished by the external acknowledgement of supervisors and peers, these five factors deeply influence the relationship between the employee and the job.

Motivation is complex and is strongly affected by individual differences. Yet because the library is only as good as the staff providing the service, library managers must give due thought and consideration to creating an organizational climate that will foster staff growth and development, helping each and every individual to progress toward personal and professional self-worth.

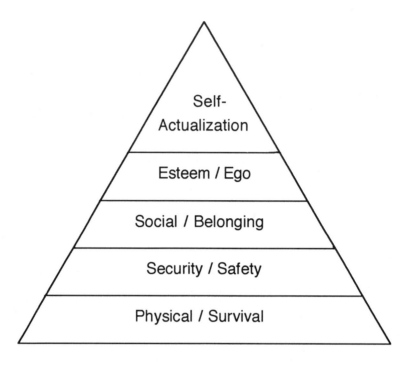

Fig. 5.1. Maslow's Hierarchy of Needs.

PERSONNEL FUNCTIONS

Although theories and principles provide a framework upon which to hang practical ideas and activities, the latter will validate or negate the most widely accepted theory. Personnel functions are necessarily detailed and specific, focusing on consistency and fairness in application. They are undergirded by the policies discussed above.

Personnel functions are necessarily tied to the expectations of employees with regard to their own jobs. The following five expectations are stated as generalizations—some employees desire more and some less—but they can be a valuable common denominator for managers to keep in mind when pondering what employees want.

- Make sure supervisor and employee both understand what is expected of the worker. In other words, "What is my job?"

- Leave the employee alone. "Having given me a job to do, leave me alone and let me do it."

- Give help if the employee asks for it. "Create an atmosphere in which I feel it is safe to ask questions."

- Tell the employee how he or she did. "How am I doing? Help me to improve."

- Reward the employee accordingly. "While I appreciate praise, talk is cheap; I see rewards tied to my performance as an indication of sincerity."[7]

Given these assumptions and expectations, jobs can be designed and employees recruited with a responsible prognosis for success.

Recruitment and Hiring

Before recruitment can be initiated, both position and job descriptions need to be developed or, if they are already in place, reviewed or revised. For purposes of this discussion, the *job* description shall be defined as outlining the parameters of a general category, such as Librarian I or Clerk-Typist I, that will be applicable to a range of possible positions. The *position* description, however, is very specific to a particular post and the individual who will fill it, such as community librarian, head of the Alpha branch library (classified as a Librarian I), or circulation clerk (classified as a Clerk-Typist I).

Job descriptions go hand in hand with establishing salary schedules, whereas position descriptions offer starting salaries that correlate to these schedules. Job descriptions are more broadly written and will likely remain in effect for longer periods of time. The position description, on the other hand, should be revised annually during the performance review so that it remains an accurate description of what is actually taking place from day to day.

In the case of a new position, a new description must be written; in refilling an existing position, the position description should be analyzed by the incumbent before the job is vacated. If changes are to be made, the time to make those changes is before recruitment begins.

Affirmative action rules and regulations are key factors in hiring in the public sector. Great care needs to be taken so that equal opportunity is given to all candidates for a position. If the community has an affirmative action officer, the language of the advertisement can be passed by that individual to ensure that it is in compliance. In addition, a procedure should be established so that a set of criteria is developed that will be applied by the search and screen committee to each application. If a point system can be created, the prescreening stage is greatly simplified.

Once prescreening of applications is completed, the finalists (or "short list") are considered again in anticipation of inviting one or more for interview. Occasionally, a pre-interview is conducted at a conference or over the telephone before the applicant is invited for a formal interview; if so, a list of questions to ask of each applicant should be developed in order to maintain consistency.

When the finalists to be interviewed have been determined and invitations have been extended, the list of questions should be reconsidered, adjusted, and enlarged upon as appropriate. Interviews typically consist of introductory remarks by the chair of the search committee concerning the organization and the position, followed by questions of the candidate, an opportunity for the candidate to ask questions, and an explanation of benefits. A rating system can also be applied to this process, and notes should be taken. References must be checked at some point in this sequence and, in acknowledgment of the busy schedules of those persons listed as references, can appropriately be deferred until a final selection has been made.

Once the new employee has been hired, it is important to provide a period of orientation. There is, of course, the typical completion of forms, issuance of keys, and so forth. More important, however, is an organized period (perhaps of several weeks) during which the new employee works at various job assignments in different areas and/or locations of library service. This broad introduction provides a context for the new employee that is vital to understanding where the individual position fits into the overall organizational structure.

Evaluation and Performance Appraisal

Every employee is entitled to performance review. In the case of new hires, there is normally a probation period of six months for support staff and twelve months for professional staff. If the position falls under civil service regulations, these time periods are predetermined.

Although some may view performance review as a negative experience, the concept of "entitlement" is definitely preferred. Every employee deserves feedback concerning his or her performance. The review should not only evaluate the past year's activities—in the context of personal goals and objectives—but also discuss and determine the goals and objectives for the next year. Thus, the performance review is an opportunity for growth and planning rather than a stereotypical "blame and praise" session.

Careful consideration needs to be given to this objective-setting process. If an objective cannot be met or if no way of meeting it can be envisioned, it should be withdrawn, lest it stand as a reminder of implied inefficiency and defuse employee motivation. Objectives should be important, worthwhile, and achievable if they are to be useful benchmarks for performance review.[8]

When carried out correctly, performance review serves several important purposes:

- It creates and maintains satisfactory levels of performance.

- It identifies needed improvements and areas for growth.

- It creates a dialogue between supervisor and employee in the context of goal- and objective-setting.

- It provides an opportunity to sit back and assess the job and how it may have changed over the past year—resulting in a revision of the position description.

- It establishes criteria for suitable rewards for excellence (and initiates a process for dealing with inadequate performance).

Performance review is an important pillar supporting the structure of personnel management. It needs to be taken seriously and be given adequate thought and attention.

Salaries and Other Rewards

Librarianship is admittedly not a highly paid profession—a marketing problem that needs to be addressed. Despite these financial limitations, however, the service orientation of the work attracts many dedicated and capable individuals. Regardless of actual dollars, the perception of "fairness" is key to establishing a system of rewards. Fairness comes into play both in terms of one position vis-à-vis other comparable positions (the issue of comparable worth) and as it relates to value received relative to value performed (does my salary reflect the excellence of my work?).

Salaries and Comparable Worth

The notion that each employee's work, although important and unique, has parallels with work performed by employees in other public units and departments is called "comparable worth." In recent years, many studies and court cases have addressed the issue of comparable worth in an effort to incorporate that elusive quality of "fairness." In order to compare jobs that are outwardly different in mission and intent, specific job tasks and responsibilities are delineated and used as the basis of analysis. Affirmative action and gender-related issues have provided much of the impetus driving comparable worth, and library workers frequently will find pursuing this strategy to their financial advantage.

Once base salary schedules have been developed, many libraries attempt to reward excellence—or provide negative feedback for poor performance—by establishing merit raise increases. Some criteria-based scale should be developed prior to such an exercise in order to bring the perception of fairness into the process. In order to administer such a process, managers need to collect documentation from staff members concerning how well job-related goals and objectives have been met during the year being considered, what continuing education opportunities and professional association activities have been pursued, and any other relevant data. The results of the exercise should be fed back to each employee during the annual performance review.

In the public sector, salaries are often tied to a system such as that administered by the Civil Service Commission. Salary schedules are established for each type of position, and annual raises are structured so as to equitably affect salaries "across the board." When layoffs occur, they are generally applied according to seniority or length of service. Not infrequently, unions are also part of the picture, and salary increases are negotiated on an annual basis.

This egalitarian approach may foster a feeling of security in employees, but it is difficult to incorporate in the effort to motivate and/or reward employees. When this situation exists, the creativity of the library's management is challenged to provide alternative reward structures. What alternatives are possible? There are many possibilities, with countless more to be imagined. Examples of these alternatives include:

- Paid education and/or continuing education
- An office with a window or a better view
- A more prestigious job title
- A special project
- Job sharing
- Job exchange

Some of these examples represent "horizontal ladders," as opposed to the vertical ladders of promotion and advancement. The underlying concept is one of enrichment through a change in responsibilities, environment, and/or opportunities. These approaches can be very effective as motivators and as rewards for excellence—valuable to the administrator at any time, but particularly welcome during periods of economic constraint.

Coaching, Disciplinary Measures, and Termination

Excellence is the goal that every manager seeks, but the converse is also present—the employee who proves to be inadequate for the work assigned. For some employees performing at low levels, the negative reinforcement of little or no salary increase, coupled with candid performance review, may be sufficient. In every case, however, the process of coaching should be the first intervention attempted.

Coaching is a term derived from athletics and, as such, brings with it certain mental imagery as well as process. Coaching includes analysis of performance, setting of mutually acceptable goals and objectives for change, monitoring of progress, and periodic assessment. Each coaching session should be thoroughly documented and the reports placed in the employee's personnel file. This documentation is essential so that there is ample evidence if further disciplinary measures must be taken.

If coaching proves to be insufficient, further measures may include a letter of reprimand (also placed in the employee's file), a requirement for further education or training, suspension, and ultimately termination. If the employee belongs to a union, the union steward must be part of each session and be a partner during the entire process. Should the employee seek to appeal whatever decisions are made, the union procedures must be followed.

When termination is the outcome (whether for poor performance or through resignation or retirement), an exit interview should be held in order to seek employee ideas and perceptions regarding the organization in general and the job in particular. Exit interviews can provide a wealth of useful information for the library manager and often are a catalyst for future change.

Staff Development

One of the most important of personnel functions is the assurance of staff development—in other words, the continual maintaining and nurturing of the library's most critical (and expensive) resource. Although staff development is discussed at length later in this chapter, it is appropriate to also list it now as a vital personnel function, lest its value to the organization somehow not be fully recognized.

Antidotes for Creeping Obsolescence

A warning sign reading, "DANGER: OBSOLESCENCE IN THE MARKETPLACE" should be placed on every diploma from high school through graduate school. The notion that a course of study, whether academic or vocational/technical, prepares a person for a lifetime career is outdated and dangerous. The average "shelf life" of a degree today has been estimated at approximately five years—and it is declining. Information and knowledge change so rapidly that reliance on what has been learned as a guarantee for present and future competence is a false hope. One of the core reasons for the movement toward increased specialization in various professions is the awareness that keeping abreast of new developments is becoming more and more difficult. The attempt to assure professional quality in library service is a primary managerial challenge.

Those with professional proficiency can become either obsolete or burned-out because of some combination of individual and situational changes. These changes can occur through personal attitudes and experiences and through shifts in societal, career, or organizational expectations.

Obsolescence can be defined as less than optimal proficiency for current professional performance. An optimal level is usually based on implicit standards of effective practice as reflected in occupational expectations, demands, and constraints expressed by opinion leaders in work settings, professional associations, educational institutions, and regulatory organizations—the sum of which constitutes the current state of the art.[9] Any performance level that is not current with this state of the art can be deemed, at least in part, obsolete.

Proficiency upon completion of preservice education is presumed to be relatively sound, so obsolescence and burnout can be tied to what occurs in the staff member's work life. It is a tall order for information workers to avoid objective obsolescence and subjective burnout, remain sufficiently competent to be accountable in their positions, and enhance the joie de vivre of the work setting. Yet that is exactly what must take place if that aspect of life is to flourish.

The Art of Work

> The attainment of proficiency, the pushing of your skill with attention to the most delicate shades of excellence, is a matter of vital concern. Efficiency of a practically flawless kind may be reached naturally in the struggle for bread. But there is something beyond—a higher point, a subtle and unmistakable touch of love and pride beyond mere skill; almost an inspiration which gives to all work that finish which is almost art—which is art.
> —Joseph Conrad

How can this "art" be achieved? What is that nebulous something that delineates the professional from the person who works a 9-to-5 job? What inspires a worker to commit the time, energy, and dedication that so often is associated with the professions?

In an attempt to identify possible responses to these questions, the perspective of learning behavior proposed in this chapter is in keeping with McGregor's "Theory Y" philosophy, which contends that the average human being not only learns to accept responsibility but actually seeks it,[10] and with Knowles's theory of andragogy, which states that the adult professional learns with internal motivation in a self-directed and problem-solving manner.[11] Add to this positive view of the adult learner the individual's self-perception of personal worth and the value of work—plus a sense of commitment to that chosen work—and a portrait of a "professional" emerges. Although the professions originated in the narrow areas of law, medicine, and the ministry, the definition to be followed here will encompass that combination of positive self-perception, value, and commitment described above.

In an effort to capture a glimpse of the art of work and its relationship to a sense of professionalism, it is useful to examine Houle's five characteristics of professionalization:

1. Clarifying the defining function or functions: the mission

2. Mastery of theoretical knowledge: the information and theory that comprise the knowledge base

3. Capacity to solve problems: the application of theoretical knowledge and practical experiential wisdom

4. Use of practical knowledge: that body of knowledge that has grown out of the nature, history, scope, and processes of practical application

5. Self-enhancement: new personal dimensions of knowledge, skill, and sensitivity by the arduous study of topics not directly related to the occupation[12]

Preservice education is realistically concerned with the first and second characteristics; the rest of the points are grounded in the merging of theory and practice, of learned facts tempered by experience and living. The considerable gap between the achievement of requisite preservice education and mature professionalization must be bridged by continuing education.

CONTINUING EDUCATION
AND COMPETENCE

There is admittedly great variation in the quality of service provided by staff members. This is a result of a range of personal and social factors, but it is widely assumed that important among them is the relative rapidity with which individuals adopt new ideas and practices.[13]

Rogers and Shoemaker[14] measured how quickly people adopt an innovation and concluded that individuals are distributed along a normal bell-shaped curve, with the majority in the large center and innovators and laggards at the two extremes. Those who fall near the innovator pole will most quickly and enthusiastically adopt and adapt to change. This positive relationship is heartening, but the converse must also be examined. It is correspondingly true that library workers who fall at the lower end of the bell curve are likely to resist change and consequently project less competence, negatively affecting the reputation of everyone in the profession.

Further, Houle's investigations of linkages between rate of adoption of an innovation and continuing education showed that

> a close relationship exists between rate of adoption and each of the following factors: favorable attitude toward education; favorable attitude toward science; extent of contact with people whose function it is to bring about change; amount of exposure to mass media; openness to interpersonal channels of communication; extent of general social participation; cosmopolitanism as contrasted to localism; number of years of formal education; intelligence; and degree of specialization of practice.[15]

Of course, the diversity of genetics, socialization, and experience allows for a wide range of individual approaches. But it is because individuals of lesser competence do, in fact, exist and have little inclination to meet change confidently and with interest that there has been a recent drive toward mandatory continuing education—often linked with certification and recertification.

The Issue of Competence

Is compulsion the answer? There is intense disagreement on this question. One side will argue that mandatory retraining is the best way to assure that librarians and other professionals do, in fact, participate in continuing education activities—and to the level that has been deemed the minimum to assure acceptable performance. The opposing view is that the nature of adult learning presupposes free choice, self-direction, and internal motivation; compulsion is a totally unacceptable approach.

Objectively, mandatory continuing education (as a requirement of professional certification or licensing) supports the process by which the general public is restricted from the practice of a given trade, the provision of a given service, or the use of a specific title.[16] There is no question that mandatory continuing education is a growing trend, fed by consumer pressure in some professions and by legislation in others.

There is considerable variation in the certification requirements of public librarians. Requirements for continuing education, if they exist at all, are equally inconsistent. However, the concern regarding certification and recertification is only a symptom. The real issue is competence—how to guarantee competent professional service.

It is important to recognize that education persists whether it is actively sought or not. Adults learn through formal and informal mechanisms. In library and information science, continuing education has the important role of somehow coordinating these various learning experiences, accepting the assumption that the adult is a self-directed/self-motivated/problem-solving learner and generating educational opportunities that assist librarians in enhancing their professionalization. If this andragogical perspective of the adult is to be accepted, then self-monitoring of competence, with the assistance of regular performance reviews, is the appropriate goal—regardless of whether or not there are legal mandates in place.

One of the real benefits in self-assessment and personal goal-setting is the opportunity to examine a wider range of impinging factors than is normally considered by more structured evaluative agencies or procedures. In support of this approach and as an illustration of the potential impact of anticipated change on professional development, a Delphi study (a forecasting method pioneered by Rand Corporation) that examined public library futures until the year 2000 resulted in the recommendation that librarians will need preparation in creative problem-solving, counseling, mentoring, communications technology, human relations, research and statistical skills, and community analysis.[17] Although this study was conducted more than a decade ago, time has validated the results, and forecasting data such as this can be valuable to the self-assessor. In addition, it is both reasonable and prudent for the individual self-assessor to broaden the scope of consideration to be as comprehensive as possible. This flexibility is a definite argument for the principle of self-assessment as an ongoing activity.

Some knowledge, skills, and attitudes can be taught in library school; others need the added ingredient of experience. The issue is fairly clear: Preservice education cannot be expected to provide more than the basic foundation upon which to build a satisfying and productive career. It is the professional's obligation to update and expand upon the original base of knowledge, skills, and attitudes.

Continuing education is not a luxury or an optional activity; it is a survival mechanism that serves as insurance against occupational obsolescence and attitudinal burnout. Moreover, because continuing education can be tailored by each individual to accommodate personal requirements in terms of content and format, the opportunities for growth and development have virtually no limits.

Each individual's response depends on how he or she perceives the world. If a person's perception of the work life is one of growth, creativity, and opportunity, then that person is almost certain to be enthusiastic about continuing education and career development. Conversely, if the perception is one of stagnation, lack of mobility, and overwhelming change, then frustration and disinterest are likely results. As with other aspects of life, the glass through which the world is viewed can be cloudy, clear, rosy, or blurred. Fortunately, each individual has the power to influence this worldview, and an active involvement in the continuation of education through some means, whether formal or otherwise, can be a powerful catalyst. The ability of education to serve as an agent of change is profound.

Continuing education is more than a hedge against obsolescence and disenchantment; in its finest forms it becomes an impetus to personal growth and expanded expertise. Such a result is, of course, an invaluable benefit to the library as an organization and to the profession as a whole. There is no guarantee against mistakes, nor against the dreaded obsolescence or burnout. What is virtually guaranteed is that without continuing education, these spectres will haunt the information worker.

STAFF DEVELOPMENT AND ENRICHMENT

The broad concepts of continuing education, when linked directly to organizational involvement and goals, often become more narrowly defined as staff development. Opportunities for staff development differ in a variety of aspects, such as length of offering, place, target audience, and program developer.

Continuing education decisions made by an individual for personal career growth will frequently result in attendance at events produced by colleges and universities, private vendors, library systems, or professional associations. However, when the library and all of its employees are seeking continuing education and staff training and enrichment are the goals, the approach changes, and on-site expertise in program development may be less available. Therefore, the following discussion focuses on the "how-tos" of program planning at the institutional level and the various opportunities for staff enrichment that are more organizational than educational in the initial stages.

The Employment Setting as Classroom

The central educational task of any employing institution is to improve the quality of its product or service.[18] With respect to libraries, this task may be addressed in several ways. First, the library and/or library system may pay all or part of the expense of a continuing education program provided by an outside source. This program may be held off-site and attended by individual staff members, based upon personal self-assessment, or it can be a "packaged" program that is brought into the library setting for many or all of the staff. Management philosophy is also a fundamental ingredient; some administrations will only fund continuing education that has direct application to present duties, whereas others encourage educational pursuits that enhance employees' future career development.

However, the fact remains that education is viewed as secondary to service.[19] Service improvement is an expected outcome, and in times of financial constraint monies for education will be eliminated more readily than funds for services. This decision is frequently a short-term Band-aid solution with negative long-term implications, but management priorities are often skewed away from emphasis on continuing education.

When an instructional program is sponsored by an institution for its own staff, it is usually defined as in-service training. Whether the instruction is delivered by an outside provider or by local talent, in person or via telecommunications or other media formats, the content is likely to be job-specific and practical, with little theoretical base. In order to provide more depth, a well-planned in-service program should be designed, with some theoretical foundation built into that design.[20]

Program Design

The design of in-service programs follows the same general sequence as the planning model: philosophy or mission, needs assessment, goals, measurable objectives and actions, and evaluation. A quality design cannot be thrown together on short notice. Professional program planners may appear to be able to accomplish this feat, but such a result is deceptive, as experience and expertise are overriding contributing elements. For the amateur, the process takes time and should be tackled by a broadly based committee in much the same manner as the planning process.

The *philosophy,* or *mission,* is the first and primary consideration. Why is staff development to be done? Why is continuing education important? What position does the library take in relation to employee continuing education? What administrative supports can the employee expect, specifically in terms of released time and funding? This organizational perspective must be clearly understood and stated before any further progress is attempted.

Once a firm philosophical base has been laid, a carefully constructed *needs assessment,* or *situational analysis,* forms the parameters of the design. The internal and external environments are evaluated to determine individual competence and library effectiveness in meeting service responsibilities to the community—and what standards should be met in these regards. Once the gaps between present and desirable levels are identified—and these needs could be limitations in terms of personal or institutional knowledge, skills, and/or attitudes— then goals and objectives can be developed in order to bridge those gaps.

In determining needs, data must be gathered from a variety of sources through a menu of mechanisms, such as research of secondary sources followed by collection of primary data. Primary data, as in the planning process, can be gathered through questionnaires, interviews, and observation, plus the addition of performance appraisal. Diverse methods of soliciting data will produce a more well-rounded information product, which will, in turn, lead to better defined goals and objectives.

The *setting of goals* to address needs can be a challenging activity. Each goal should be related to one or more needs, be tailored to the targeted audience, and have sufficient scope so that it offers a continual reach. Each objective must be measurable, with a target completion date and designation of responsibility, and move the library closer to the related goal. For example, if the needs assessment has discovered 1) that schools in the area provide considerable hands-on experience on microcomputers as part of the curriculum; 2) that an increasing number of homes are investing in these personal computers; 3) that the library has no microcomputers; and 4) that the staff has a low level of computer literacy, then a goal may well be to increase staff computer literacy in anticipation of providing a new service.

Objectives could include:

- Purchase a microcomputer by August 1

- Initiate a basic computer literacy in-service seminar for all staff by September 1

- Provide x hours of hands-on time to each employee by December 1

- Announce the new microcomputer access service to the public on January 1

All *action plans*—which are also measurable and time-oriented—are tied directly to objectives. The accomplishment of a series of actions should fulfill an objective and contribute to implementation of the program.

Returning to our example: In order for the in-service seminar to take place, decisions have to be made, such as: When and where will it occur? Who will instruct? What content should be covered? How will the audience be determined? What expenses is the library willing to incur? How many seminars will there be? How many participants should be in each seminar? Once these decisions are made, the nitty-gritty logistical details can be spelled out, and the responsibility for each detail should be assigned. This practical phase should not be underestimated; it takes staff time, and time is money.

As with planning, *evaluation* that both monitors the process and provides a summary analysis is an integral component of program design. Monitoring is crucial in order to ascertain whether activities are on schedule, whether anything has been omitted, or whether a new direction should be charted. The summary analysis determines elements of success and areas of shortfall, important data that can be used in designing the next program.

Creativity and Horizontal Opportunities

Although the in-service program is a commonly used and frequently effective mechanism for staff development, it is not the only one. Too often, library managers equate staff development with a produced event. However, there are other creative possibilities; options are limited only by the imagination, and program design as a process can be the structure upon which to build any type of educational opportunity.

Particularly in periods of economic uncertainty and retrenchment, which come and go for all institutions, there is typically decreasing opportunity to provide promotions and upward mobility that are so deserved by many staff members. There is often less turnover in existing positions because of economic insecurity, and new positions are often frozen or cancelled, resulting in fewer advertised positions. What can then be done for the staff member who would be promoted were conditions more favorable? What can be done to stimulate continued motivation and enthusiasm in as many employees as possible? The strategies to be described can be viewed as horizontal ladders—new and challenging experiences that can occur laterally within the organization and that add spice to a familiar routine.

Job Sharing. Two staff members with complementary personalities and expertise can readily share a single position (if both wish to work part-time) or two positions (if full-time employment is desired by both). The opportunity to enjoy a range of responsibilities and challenges and to work as a team sharing ideas and problems can be exciting and provide a boost to job satisfaction. Complementary (not necessarily similar) personalities are required so that the two individuals can work well together with a minimum of friction and a maximum amount of cooperation.

Job Exchange. Too often, technical services and public service librarians do not leave their private worlds and consequently have a distorted impression of how the rest of the library operates, particularly in large library situations. Having staff members exchange positions for a brief time can be beneficial to the library functionally and can create an impetus for high morale. It would be most useful if every library employee stood at least temporarily in the shoes of every colleague and learned the joys and frustrations to be found in each position and how all the library operations intersect in the effort to provide excellent service.

A more expanded version is the exchange between libraries, either locally or at some distance (even internationally). This can be a truly enlightening experience, as it is human nature to conclude that all libraries operate in the same way as one's own. The length of the exchange can be as short as a day or as long as one or several years. In either case, what is learned can be an invaluable opportunity and career stimulant.

Special Projects. Being assigned to short-term committees, task forces, and projects can be a welcome break in established patterns of work. Such special duty can be intensely challenging, freeing creative energies that would otherwise lie dormant. But there is a caution, too. If the reports or other products and recommendations that are generated by these groups and/or projects are not taken seriously or are ignored by management, or if thoughtful and considered feedback does not return to the employees involved, then the morale problem can be worse than before. It should follow that management that is progressive enough to initiate this type of innovative staff development activity would be wise enough to follow through, but this is not always the case.

Reorganization. The typical organizational chart is a hierarchical structure, and communication flows downward, with some upward movement. In one type of restructured model, there can be "pods," or teams, created that are based upon functions or activities; in some cases, leadership can rotate to provide managerial experience to a wider number of staff members. Such a model is often described as "orbital"—pods of activity orbiting around central management. (See fig. 4.2 on p. 67.)

Another model assumes a matrix configuration, which is also configured by activity. (See fig. 4.3 on p. 68.) Each activity has a leader, with other staff members assuming supportive roles. For example, Librarian *A* may be the lead worker on Activity 1 while performing supportive functions on Activities 2, 3, and 4. In both models, communication moves in many directions.

Such decentralized structures, in which participatory management is encouraged and facilitated, can have a very positive effect on staff sense of ownership in the decision-making process. This management style can also be a mitigating factor when promotional opportunities are scarce or when someone has been hired from outside the organization. Resentment in this latter instance can be forestalled in large part when internally eligible candidates feel involved in the administrative decision-making process, and the infusion of new perspectives that an "outside" hiring brings can be allowed to flourish. Although group decision-making initially consumes more time, the long-term benefits of generation of creative ideas, sense of involvement, and shared talents more than compensate.

Staff Development and Change

Education must equip people to change as society and technology change. The skills and knowledge needed to be productive and satisfied are changing as well; employees must learn skills in decision-making, problem-solving, creativity, communication, critical thinking, evaluation, analysis, and synthesis.[21] These skills are not job-specific; rather, they are enablers, skills that provide a strong base upon which to build further continuing education in new and unfamiliar areas. Although the explosion of information and technology will require the acquisition of new knowledge, the development of enabling skills will make new learning and implementation of what is learned that much easier.

Staff development is initiated as a response to a need for internal organizational change; an individual's continuing education may also occur as a result of personal awareness of a present or anticipated knowledge gap—which also relates to current or perceived change. Change is a powerful catalyst for stimulating educational needs; education can be the corresponding catalyst for coping effectively with change.

It is a definite challenge to flow with the rapid rate of change that society faces today. This challenge will become more profound as the rate of change intensifies, and there is certainly no indication that this rate will slow or decrease. Organizations such as libraries will need to move aggressively with whatever new services or service orientations appear to be in harmony with the shifting environment. Staff training and enrichment are important tools in the struggle to keep pace with new options and opportunities. The encouragement of employee personal continuing education planning will pay both short- and long-range organizational dividends. High morale and enthusiasm for personal and institutional goals will make adaptation and innovation more than a possibility; they will make it a probability and a one-way, no-looking-back ticket into the information age.

For Discussion

- What type of organizational pattern is present in your library?
- Does your library have a personnel policy? If you operate under a municipal policy, is there a separate policy for the library that relates to that overall policy? Are there gaps in the policy that should be addressed?
- What levels of staff are employed in your library? What is the attitude toward support staff? toward volunteers? Are volunteers regarded as "unpaid staff"?
- Consider staff attitude in your library. Even if you feel that the overall attitude is reasonably good, what can be done to enrich and empower staff, to increase morale, to nurture positive feelings?
- What can be done to improve your recruitment procedures?
- Are performance reviews done annually? tied to individual goals and objectives?
- How is discipline presently handled? Is there a process in place that includes a range of procedures from coaching through termination?
- How is continuing education viewed in your library? Are there administrative supports in place, such as work-release time, reimbursement for registration fees and/or tuition? Are employees encouraged to share with others what they have learned? Is participation in continuing education tied to salary increase and/or advancement?

Scenario Five
They're Lucky to Have a Job . . . or . . .

The Facts
Ken and Jane are recent graduates from an ALA-accredited program in a well-respected school of library and information studies.

Both had the traditional basic courses, plus added coursework in audiovisual materials, automation, and management.

Ken is enthusiastic about being involved in the information society and hopes to manage a medium-to-large public library someday.

Jane enjoys library work but cannot envision herself as a manager. She views librarianship through traditional eyes and plans to go into public service.

What Could/Would Happen If . . .
. . . the following things take place in the next decade:

- Ken actively seeks out continuing education with emphasis on management; Jane does not.
- Jane is employed by a library whose management strongly encourages continuing education and provides time and monetary incentives; Ken's library is less generous.
- Both librarians attend a library system-sponsored workshop on the public library and the information society; the instructor offers a dynamic look at change and technological development.
- A progressive school of library and information studies offers a noncredit certificate program in a variety of topic options: management, automation, youth services, preservation, archives, buildings, and bibliographic instruction. Each course to be taken lasts two days.
- Jane is offered an opportunity to chair a task force within the library with the charge to investigate a new integrated system.
- Ken applies for several director positions; he consistently comes in second.
- Both are candidates for office in the state library association.
- Both are urged to return to school for a higher degree.

NOTES

1. Fritz J. Roethlisberger and William J. Dickson, "Human Relations," in Beverly P. Lynch, ed., *Management Strategies for Libraries* (New York: Neal-Schuman Publishers, 1985), 117-118.

2. Ibid., 118-121.

3. Robert D. Stueart and Barbara B. Moran, *Library Management*, 3d ed. (Littleton, CO: Libraries Unlimited, 1987), 97-98.

4. Dana C. Rooks, *Motivating Today's Library Staff: A Management Guide* (Phoenix: Oryx Press, 1988), 22.

5. Frederick Herzberg, Bernard Mausner, and Barbara B. Snyderman, *The Motivation to Work*, 2d ed. (New York: John Wiley, 1959), 30-36.

6. Abraham H. Maslow, *Motivation and Personality* (New York: Harper & Row, 1954), 37-46.

7. Herbert S. White, *Library Personnel Management* (White Plains, NY: Knowledge Industries Publications, 1985), 126-128.

8. Ibid., 41.

9. Alan B. Knox, "The Nature and Causes of Professional Obsolescence," in Preston P. LeBreton et al., eds., *The Evaluation of Continuing Education for Professionals: A Systems View* (Seattle: University of Washington, 1979), 133.

10. Melvin J. LeBaron and Marshall Fels, "Leadership Styles, Strategies and Tactics," in Ellen Altman, ed., *Local Public Library Administration*, 2d ed. (Chicago: American Library Association, 1980), 71.

11. Malcolm S. Knowles, *The Modern Practice of Adult Education: From Pedagogy to Andragogy*, rev. ed. (Chicago: Association Press/Follett, 1980), 40-62.

12. Cyril O. Houle, *Continuing Learning in the Professions* (San Francisco: Jossey-Bass, 1980), 35, 40-49.

13. Cyril O. Houle, "Evidence for the Effectiveness of Continuing Professional Education and the Impact of Mandatory Continuing Education," in Donald E. Moore, Jr., ed., *Proceedings: Mandatory Continuing Education: Prospects and Dilemmas for Professionals* (Urbana: University of Illinois, 1976), 123.

14. E. M. Rogers and F. E. Shoemaker, *Communication of Innovations* (New York: Free Press, 1971).

15. Houle, "Evidence for the Effectiveness of Continuing Professional Education," 124.

16. Robert S. Donnelly, *Continuing Professional Education: An Appraisal* (a report for the Division of Continuing Education, University of Massachusetts at Amherst, 1977), 3.

17. Darlene E. Weingand, *Reflections of Tomorrow: Lifelong Learning and the Public Library* (Minneapolis: D.E.R.B.y Associates, 1980), 196.

18. Houle, *Continuing Learning in the Professions*, 185.

19. Ibid.

20. There are numerous works in the literature of adult education concerning program design. The reader is particularly directed to the writings of Cyril O. Houle.

21. Marvin J. Cetron, "Getting Ready for the Jobs of the Future," *The Futurist* 17:3 (June 1983), 15-22.

Directing and Leading

Directing and leading are two major components of management that are often inaccurately viewed as synonymous. Although competence in these areas is an important attribute of the successful manager, it is important to recognize the differences as well as the similarities between them. This chapter will examine the permutations of directing and leading, with attention given to motivation, decision-making, and organizational communication.

DIRECTING

Directing can be defined as the managerial function that enables managers to get things done through people, both individually and in groups. Directing builds upon the skills of library employees by guiding and coordinating them toward the library's goals and objectives.[1]

Because every library is organized in some configuration, it follows that the directing function operates in close harmony with this organizational structure. However, regardless of the exact structure, there must necessarily be several levels of management:

Top management, which typically includes the library's director, assistant or associate director, business manager, and any other members of the administrative team that operate at the highest level. A large library may have a management team that includes a branch chief, a chief of central library operations, a head of technical services, and so forth. In a small library, the director may operate in a solo environment.

Middle management, which includes the managers of subunits. These individuals may be department heads or branch heads in a larger organization. The smaller library will have fewer (if any) off-site outlets, and middle managers may well be those who are in charge of technical and public services.

Supervisors, or "front-line" managers, who direct the activities of all individuals who are not in management positions. In large libraries, a supervisor may be in charge of a large number of staff; in smaller organizations, there may be only one or several employees to be supervised. Because supervisors are closest to individual employees, they strongly influence both performance and job satisfaction—and ultimately employee morale.

Each of these management levels has unique responsibilities to the overall administration of the library. Top management officials are primarily concerned with policy affecting the entire organization and charting directions for the future. The management style forged at this highest level frequently permeates the organization and sets the tone for the other levels of management. Middle managers serve two interrelated purposes: governing the operations of the areas for which they have responsibility and serving as liaisons between top management and the supervisory level. Supervisors, as links with most individual employees, often provide the most practical and day-to-day (if not hour-to-hour!) direction.

Although the scope of the directing function varies with each level of management, the basic tenets still apply, and all managers, regardless of level, should be knowledgeable in strategies of good directing so that a productive and nurturing environment can be created.

Theory X and Theory Y

Much has been written in the management literature concerning the two theories developed by Douglas McGregor in the 1950s. These two theories, Theory X and Theory Y, reflect the two poles of a continuum illustrating assumptions regarding human nature.[2] The assumptions undergirding Theory X include the following:

- Human beings have an inherent dislike of work and will avoid it if at all possible.

- The average person is passive, preferring to be directed, and avoids responsibility; there is relatively little ambition, and security is highly desirable.

- Because they dislike work, people need to be controlled with punishment, including coercion and threats, to get them to perform adequately.

Obviously, Theory X is an extremely pessimistic view and represents the negative, more traditional pole. Yet there are managers who see their employees through Theory X eyes and prefer to manage from a hierarchical and tightly controlled perspective. Although this emphasis on authority can range anywhere from the extreme negative pole to somewhere near the midpoint on the continuum, it is important to recognize that this approach to management does exist and can be a powerful influence on the organizational climate.

The other pole, which represents the attitudes of a changing work force, is illustrated by Theory Y. These assumptions include the following:

- The activity called work, in terms of mental and physical effort, is natural to the human being.

- Rather than requiring external control and threat of punishment, the worker employs self-direction and self-control and relates to organizational objectives to which s/he is committed.

- This commitment is tied to rewards linked with their achievement; internal rewards, such as self-actualization and ego satisfaction, are of most significance.

- The worker will seek out responsibility and is capable of more intellectual potential than is generally utilized.

- Imagination, ingenuity, and creativity are widely, not narrowly, distributed in the population.

Theory Y represents the positive pole, implying that human nature is dynamic, creative, and highly capable of growth and increasing responsibility. The implications here are that the organizational climate must be nurturing rather than coercive, empowering rather than controlling. Managers who subscribe to Theory Y face continuous challenges to their own creativity in developing and sustaining this empowering organizational climate.

Although these are theories, they inform managerial thinking and encourage managers to reflect upon their own assumptions regarding the employees in the organization. Further, these theories are substantiated in large part by prevailing thought in adult education literature, particularly through the writing of Malcolm S. Knowles and his theory of andragogy.[3] (Andragogy contends that adults are self-directed and problem-solving, utilizing experience in the process.)

Clearly, the function of directing is not a simple one, and it is deeply influenced by personal attitudes and philosophies—on the part of both managers and employees. Indeed, there are times when an approach at any point in the continuum may be entirely appropriate. However, in today's workplace, the assumptions of Theory Y thinking are becoming dominant as staff seek to work in an environment that encourages professional growth and development. The notion of direction has been shifting from overt control to covert empowerment. If the desire of top management is to create a Theory Y environment, it is incumbent upon them to seek out and/or develop middle managers and supervisors who will promulgate this managerial policy.

LEADERSHIP

Management may, or may not, be the soulmate of leadership. Directing, too, may be rooted in leadership, or it may be mired in administrative detail. In other words, there is no guarantee that any given manager is also a leader—or that a leader necessarily has managerial capabilities. If the library were located in Camelot, all managers would also be leaders; in the real world, this cannot be assumed to be true.

Phases of Leadership

What, then, is leadership? Historically, thinking concerning leadership has moved through three distinct phases:

1. *The Trait Phase.* This approach emphasized the examination of leader characteristics in an attempt to identify a set of universal traits that would enable a person to be effective in all situations. Over time, lack of conclusive evidence prompted researchers to move away from this approach.

2. *The Behavioral Phase.* Research conducted from the late 1940s to the early 1960s suggested that high consideration and high structure were prime dimensions of leader behavior. Eventually, other research concluded that different combinations of consideration and structure were found to be more effective. Therefore, no single leadership style was deemed universally effective, and research moved toward yet another approach.

3. *The Situational Phase.* Current leadership research focuses largely on situation, analyzing interrelationships among leaders and subordinates in terms of the circumstances in which these individuals find themselves. Leadership styles may range from unilateral decision-making to simple facilitation of a group.[4]

Many factors will influence the situation, including the pressures of time and personalities, and it is entirely normal for the leader to swing between highly directive and highly participatory approaches, depending upon those situational factors. Overlaying the situation, however, is the leader's personal style and the managerial strategies with which he or she feels comfortable. The sum of situation and personal style becomes that amorphous entity called "leadership style."

Characteristics of Leadership

Another current leadership model proposes a core list of four characteristics, with a superstructure of eight functions built upon it.[5] The four characteristics include:

A clear vision of what the organization might become

The ability to communicate the vision to others

The ability to motivate others to work toward the vision

The ability to "work the system" to get things done

Using these four characteristics as a foundation, the following superstructure can be erected:

1. *Creating the vision*: Constructing a crystal-clear mental picture of what the group should become and then transmitting this vision to the minds of others.

2. *Developing the team*: Assembling a group of highly qualified people who are jointly responsible for achieving the group's goals.

3. *Clarifying the values*: Identifying the organizational values and communicating them through words and actions.

4. *Positioning*: Developing an effective strategy for moving the group toward the vision.

5. *Communicating*: Achieving a common understanding with others by using all modes of communication effectively.

6. *Empowering*: Motivating others by raising them to their "better selves."

7. *Coaching*: Helping others develop the skills needed for achieving excellence.

8. *Measuring*: Identifying the critical success factors associated with the group's operation and gauging progress on the basis of these factors.

Each of these facets should be viewed as a continuum of potential, and every manager aspiring to the role of leader needs to realize that placement on each of the eight continua will fluctuate from day to day. In other words, on a scale of 1 to 10, a manager may rate a "6" on clarifying and positioning but only a "3" on communicating and coaching today, yet rise to a "9" in the communication area tomorrow. Both true abilities and perception of ability shift in accordance with self-confidence and self-image, so a sense of humanness and latitude in expectations is essential to placing leadership potential in perspective.

Effectiveness and Competence

Effectiveness must be viewed apart from leadership style; every manager has a leadership style, but every manager is not a leader. Warren Bennis, in his research seeking to identify areas of leadership competence, defined four competency areas:

Management of Attention: the ability to draw others to oneself; to communicate an extraordinary focus of commitment; to enroll others in one's vision.

Management of Meaning: the ability to communicate one's vision; to move beyond explanation or clarification to the creation of meaning.

Management of Trust: the ability to project reliability, constancy, and focus.

Management of Self: the ability to know one's skills and strengths, and deploy them effectively; to learn from and use mistakes, seeing them not as failures but as the next step; to view worry as an obstacle to clear thinking and accept the possibility of being wrong.[6]

These competences lead to the growth of empowerment in an organization, nurturing energy and creativity on the part of staff. When effective leadership is present in a library, there are four observable results:

- People feel significant, believing that they make a difference to the success of the organization.

- Learning and competence matter; failure is not a negative but an opportunity to gain feedback that informs what to do next.

- People are part of a community, feeling that they are members of a team.

- Work is exciting, stimulating, challenging, and fun; staff are "pulled" rather than "pushed" toward achieving goals.[7]

This sense of empowerment flows out of Theory Y assumptions about people—belief that dedication and love of work are part of the human condition, if leadership is present to nurture that growth. Facilitation, not control, is key to managerial philosophy, and quality of service is the inevitable outcome. Employee motivation is internal and need not be managed by external hope of reward.

MOTIVATING

In motivational theory, "motivation" is defined as a technique or concept that influences the actions of an individual by integrating personal goals with organizational goals in an environment that can provide a common ground for these competing needs. Yet it must be acknowledged that each individual's environment extends far beyond the workplace to include personal life, family and friends, society, and miscellaneous outside factors.[8]

Each employee is a three-dimensional human being, with myriad "hats" to wear. Further, the patterns of human development discussed in chapter 3 strongly affect an individual's motivation during the different stages of life and need to be taken into consideration.

Because of these various influences, motivation cannot be regarded as a linear process. It often is, however, and several myths have arisen concerning the effort to motivate employees. Some of these myths include:

- *An unmotivated employee does not perform as well as a motivated employee.* This myth does not take levels of knowledge and skill into account—in other words, an unmotivated employee may have a high skill level, producing an acceptable rate of productivity, whereas a motivated employee having inadequate skills (and needing training) may not. Therefore, there needs to be a blend of motivation and the ability to do the job.

- *Motivating staff is solely the responsibility of management.* In fact, management is charged with providing an environment that offers opportunity for motivation and growth; the employee has a responsibility to take advantage of this environment. (As discussed in chapter 3, the adult is ultimately self-directed.)

- *All employees can be motivated.* As mentioned above, each employee is influenced by numerous factors, and at particular periods of life, motivation may not be possible or may be limited.

- *There are "lazy" employees.* (This is a myth based on a Theory X view of people.) Rather, such employees may be in an unmotivated phase of life, the job may not be a good fit, or some may be discouraged.[9]

Moving beyond these misconceptions, there are two basic types of motivation: external and internal. External rewards were introduced in the last chapter; the nurturing of internal desires for excellence was discussed above in terms of leadership. Two researchers have postulated theories of motivation that have gained credibility over time, theories that relate to both internal and external motivation.

Abraham Maslow's Hierarchy of Human Needs

Maslow's hierarchy is based upon the theory that self-motivation is integral to fulfillment of human needs.[10] This theory does not deny the effect of external rewards, as several of the levels in the hierarchy can obviously be influenced externally. As briefly discussed in chapter 5, the levels Maslow proposed (see fig. 5.1 on p. 78.) fall into two categories: lower-order and higher-order. The two bottom levels—physical/survival and security/safety—are essential to human life, and these must be satisfied to a certain degree before thought can be given to the higher-order needs. Physical and security needs are so compelling that when threats are present, all human attention is drawn to correcting the situation.

Once these basic levels have stabilized, higher-level needs can be addressed. Higher needs include social/belonging, esteem/ego, and self-actualization. The human being is fundamentally social and searches for gratification of these interpersonal needs. Again, remembering the three-dimensional perspective, it is relatively clear that in order to attain wholeness, not only the soundness of the body but also the wellness of the mind and soul are critical to total personality integration.

When this integration is comfortable, it is possible to leap for the pinnacle of self-actualization—depicted as pointed probably because it can be attained temporarily but is difficult to perch upon indefinitely. Self-actualization is the driving need to reach one's own potential, to use it in such a way as to achieve the best one is capable of achieving.

Maslow's approach focuses on the employee; the next researcher concentrates on the job setting.

Herzberg's Job Satisfiers and Dissatisfiers

As also introduced in chapter 5, Frederick Herzberg asked two questions in his research on motivation.[11] These questions were:

- Think of a work-related incident that happened in your life that made you feel very negative and tell me why it made you feel negative.

- Think of a work-related incident that happened in your life that made you feel good and tell me why it made you feel good.

The results of this research produced two lists. The five most common factors resulting in negative feelings were policy and administration, supervision, relationship with supervisor, work conditions, and salary. The five most common factors producing positive feelings were achievement, recognition, the work itself, responsibility, and advancement.

In the first list, it is the absence of affirmation and good relationships that produces the negative feelings. None of these factors is intrinsically negative. In addition, these factors are external in character—and therefore readily controllable by the manager.

Conversely, the second list contains internal factors that reflect the individual's response to the work environment. These positive feelings can be elicited by the manager by the creation of a nurturing climate with opportunities for growth.

The library manager, in seeking to motivate employees, must create a working environment in which each employee has and perceives the opportunity to grow, to develop, and to reach for higher levels of achievement without being caught by the snares of bureaucracy. Internal satisfaction is the goal, but external rewards can successfully contribute to this satisfaction when carefully and sensitively added to the mix. Decision-making ability can make the difference in knowing when and how to develop motivation strategies.

DECISION-MAKING

Peter Drucker has said, "A decision is a judgment. It is a choice between alternatives. It is rarely a choice between right and wrong. It is at best a choice between 'almost right' and 'probably wrong'—but much more often a choice between two courses of action neither of which is probably more nearly right than the other."[12] This statement highlights the emotional baggage that all too frequently accompanies decision-making—baggage that clutters the mental field with the fear of "making a mistake" or "making the wrong decision." This fear can render the manager powerless to decide—a condition that is, in itself, a decision (of inaction).

The appropriate perspective to take is to view a decision and its aftermath as data for the next decision to be made—nothing more, nothing less. Removing the emotional context can free the manager to fully explore the alternatives without the twin specters of fear and blame hovering nearby. Unfortunately, Western culture has perpetuated the fear/blame approach to decision-making. This mold must be broken if decision-making is to reach maximum effectiveness.

The process of decision-making involves a series of steps: defining the problem; analyzing it; establishing criteria by which it can be evaluated; identifying alternative solutions; selecting the "best" one; implementing it; and, finally, evaluating the results. This process involves three phases: 1) intelligence—identifying the problem and seeking information concerning the problem; 2) design—determining the possible courses of action and analyzing them as potential solutions; and 3) choice—selecting and implementing a course of action.[13] This is a formalization of what is, for many, an intuitive process. Yet even on the subjective plane, these basic steps are typically present.

Participative Decision-Making

When groups are involved in the decision-making process, the basic sequence of steps remains the same, but the process changes significantly because of group dynamics. There are both advantages and disadvantages to participative management, but the pros definitely outweigh the cons. On the negative side, the process does eat up time, as everyone must have an opportunity to express comments along the way. However, the collective "ownership" of the final result that occurs by virtue of everyone's having been involved is so significant that this extended time commitment in the short term is well worth the investment; in the long term, the expended time is reclaimed because of the group's commitment.

When a group is to be involved, clarity of purpose is essential. The group is entitled to know which of these several models would be in effect:

- The group discusses options and communicates information to the manager, who makes the decision.

- Individual members of the group are polled by the manager for information, and the manager makes the decision.

- The group discusses options and makes recommendations to the manager, who still makes the decision.

- The group is charged with examining alternatives and making the decision.

The decision-making process, like leadership, is closely tied to the situation at hand. There are at least three classes of outcomes that bear on the process to reach the decision:

- The quality or rationality of the decision

- The acceptance or commitment on the part of subordinates to execute the decision effectively

- The amount of time required to make the decision[14]

In other words, if it is a decision having wide-ranging ramifications, if group acceptance is a key to success, and if there is sufficient time available, then group decision-making is highly recommended. When different situational factors, such as an extremely short time line, are in effect, more traditional decision-making may be indicated.

The process of participative management through shared decision-making improves morale, stresses a team approach, keeps individuals aware, and provides a forum for free discussion of ideas and thoughts.[15] It is part of the overall attempt to empower employees and create that environment where individual growth and creativity are fostered and encouraged. Yet it should be recognized that the process is dependent upon patterns of communication that exist in the organization; facilitating this communication will greatly enhance the decision-making effort.

ORGANIZATIONAL COMMUNICATION

The content of organizational communication typically flows from the top down because organizations traditionally have been governed in a hierarchical manner. Other strategies for organizational structure were presented in chapter 4, and communication patterns will necessarily follow the structure that is created. However, within the library's selected management structure, organizational communication will still be dependent in large part upon the skills of the individuals who are communicating.

What are the skills that support the structure of organizational communication? These skills are varied and include the following:

- Nonverbal behavior
- Listening
- Speaking: one-on-one and one-to-many
- Writing

These skills, used individually or in combination, flow through the organizational structure. Direction and leadership must be communicated; it is through these skills that communication either takes place or is diverted.

Nonverbal Behavior

Researchers have distinguished several dimensions of nonverbal behavior:

- *Kinesics*—the way we use our bodies, head, arms, legs, etc.

- *Proxemics*—the way we use interpersonal space; the distance we stand from another person

- *Paralanguage*—how we say something: the pitch, rate, loudness, and inflection of our speech

- *Chronemics*—the way we time our verbal exchanges[16]

Each of these dimensions can be eloquent in transmitting information to others. It is not uncommon for a verbal transaction to present one message while nonverbal cues are communicating quite a different message. Many confusing organizational efforts at transmitting information can be traced to situations in which two or more messages are actually in process. Whether the transaction is one-on-one or one-to-many, nonverbal cues can be powerful, and this power needs to be recognized.

In addition, there are cultural permutations rooted in ethnic heritage that may be totally outside the experience of members of other cultures—and therefore not necessarily perceived or, if perceived, not accurately understood. Consequently, it is imperative that extra care be taken in terms of organizational communication when ethnic diversity is present.

Attending Skills. Part of nonverbal communication but also a basic communication strategy, attending (or paying attention) to the message of the other person testifies that one is listening actively. There are several skills that can be practiced in order to attend to messages more effectively:

> *Eye contact.* Looking at the person during the transmission of a message indicates both interest and the desire to truly communicate. Timing of eye contact can be tricky, as too long and too short a time can pose some difficulties. Whether one is the sender or receiver of the message, if eye contact persists too long, it may be perceived as aggressiveness or an attempt to dominate. Conversely, if the timing of eye contact is too brief, it may be perceived as evasiveness and lack of confidence. If this seems tricky, it is—and practice is the only way to determine what is most effective.
>
> In addition, the earlier discussion concerning cultural differences must be reinforced here. There are definitely cultural mandates concerning the length of eye contact—or whether eye

contact is appropriate at all. Eye contact is all bound up with concepts of respect, and any lack of contact should not be misinterpreted as somehow lacking in openness or interest.

Inclining one's head, smiling. These nonverbal responses indicate that active listening is in process and encourages the other person to proceed with the message. Such behavior does not guarantee agreement with the message content, but it does validate the interaction. Conversely, an impassive face or constant shifting of one's body suggests boredom, disinterest, or even hostility.

Body posture. Shifting of the body is only one indicator of disinterest; other movements (or lack of movement) such as slumping, crossed arms, or immobility can convey such signals as well. However, leaning slightly toward the speaker carries a sense of expectation and interest.

The voice. Listed earlier as "paralanguage," the qualities of the voice can be controlled in terms of loudness/softness, high/low pitch, fast/slow rate of speech, rhythm, emphasis, and fluency. Variety can be achieved by changing the pitch and inflection, the pace, and the volume, and by inserting pauses in appropriate places. (There are those individuals who are afraid to pause because another speaker might step into the silence created, but pauses can be very effective punctuation marks.) Voice quality and resonance are determined by the formation of vowel sounds and the use of the upper throat, mouth, and nose. Tonal quality is controlled by the vowels, and the relative tenseness/relaxation of the jaw and throat greatly affect these sounds. Voice coaches generally focus their attentions in this area, and results can be quite dramatic. Articulation through the precise use of consonants requires conscious use of lips, tongue, and palate; distinct articulation lends authority and presence to the voice. Projection of the voice is governed by breathing and a relaxed throat. If adequate breath, resonance, some prolongation of vowel sounds, and distinct articulation are combined, adequate projection can be achieved.[17]

In-service training can be very useful in educating employees about the various types and styles of nonverbal and intercultural communication, as well as teaching them controlled and effective use of the voice. Particularly in libraries, where interaction with the public is the mode of business and interfaces with ongoing intraorganizational exchanges, it is extremely important that all staff be aware of how to communicate in both overt and covert styles. Communication skills are all too frequently taken for granted. However, just as other physical skills are improved through practice and dedication, communication skills must also be developed consciously and with care.

Listening

One communication skill that is closely tied to nonverbal abilities is listening. In order to find out what someone (supervisor, colleague, or client) is trying to say, to understand another's point of view, or to receive information or feedback, one must become an active listener. Listening, like other communication skills, must be deliberately practiced if improvement is to occur.[18] The following hints are designed to aid in developing listening skills:

Barriers to Listening. When people "listen," often what is going on may be more appropriately defined as "hearing." In other words, sound is being emitted, sound is being received. The amount of *meaning* that is being received will vary considerably from person to person and will be governed by a series of possible barriers, such as:

- Perceiving selectively and hearing only those messages that fit one's own worldview and set of opinions.

- Making assumptions about what others are really saying.

- Giving unsolicited advice before the entire problem has been expressed.

- Being judgmental or critical and distancing oneself from the other person's point of view.

- Being defensive or arguing, particularly if one is threatened by the other person's views.

- Focusing on what one is going to say next.

Helpful Behaviors. In order to work on improving listening skills, there are certain behaviors that will aid in the process:

- Don't interrupt; let the speaker finish both sentences and the thoughts behind them. Remember that interrupting is a strategy for exercising power.

- Don't do all the talking, and try hard to stay silent.

- Wait for an answer, and don't fill in pauses.

- Don't focus on your next response while the speaker is talking; this prevents any true listening from occurring.

- Don't change the topic; this discounts the value of what the speaker is saying and is another mechanism for securing power.

- Listen for the whole message; beyond the cognitive content of the message lie the feelings of the speaker. Watch for nonverbal cues and listen for what is not said.

- Use eye contact (see above).

- Use the encouragers of nodding, smiling, saying "uh-huh."

- Check your understanding through paraphrasing and asking for clarification.

- Ask questions that probe for more detail, such as "Can you give me an example?" or "How do you feel about this?"

As suggested earlier, these behaviors can be practiced, and they provide a worthy topic for in-service training activities.

Speaking: One-on-One and One-to-Many

The act of speaking involves specific skills in addition to pleasant and convincing voice quality. These skills also can be learned. Hints related to speaking effectively include:

- Acknowledging, or restating the content of what was just said.

- Using minimal encouragers, such as "Uh-huh," "I see," and so forth.

- Pausing for effect to enhance what was just said; as with eye contact, the length of the pause needs to be practiced and appropriate timing determined.

- Asking open questions in order to encourage others to respond more fully, such as "What requirements do you have?" or "What do you think should be done?"

- Avoiding premature diagnosis of what the other person is meaning or trying to express.

- Using neutral questions that are more structured than open questions and ask specifically about situations, gaps, or helps. Examples would include: "What are you trying to understand?" or "How would this help you?" or "What problem are you having in this situation?"

- Reflecting content to demonstrate that listening has taken place; this activity is often called paraphrasing.

- Reflecting feeling is analogous to reflecting content, except that feelings are the object of this mirroring technique. An example would be, "It sounds as if you feel. . . ."

- Using closure to tactfully return the discussion to the topic at hand when it wanders off track.

- Giving instructions and directions effectively; this includes using appropriate body language, speaking in clear and specific language, asking questions to ascertain whether the message sent has been received, and observing that the person understands and can carry out the directions.

- Telling people what you are doing and why avoids unnecessary confusion.

- Engaging in confrontation when necessary. This is a difficult skill to learn for many people, but it is necessary to the "bag of tricks." There are four basic steps: describe the situation (without blame), express feelings (specifying how one feels and why), specify changes, and point out consequences (both good and bad). This is a positive strategy for dealing with conflict and avoids the negative approaches of saying nothing until one explodes or attacking the other person's character.

- Giving feedback to others, remembering to praise in public and discipline in private. It is important to be specific, give examples, suggest improvements, limit the number of suggestions, suggest rather than prescribe, and consider the needs of the receiver.

- Offering opinions and suggestions. Give advice when asked for it; if none has been requested, inquire as to whether it may be welcome.[19]

These hints affect the content of speaking and, coupled with appropriate voice modulation, can greatly enhance the communication process.

Writing

Writing is, in many ways, putting speech on paper. However, some writing is far more formal and stylized than speech, and the approach to be taken with the written word will depend in large part upon the prospective audience. As in any process of communication, the receiver (in this case, the reader) must be considered in terms of prior knowledge and experience, relationship (if any) to the author, and their actual reading ability. Aspects of style such as tone and readability should be considered.

In general terms, conciseness and simplicity are desirable attributes of any type of writing. The simple mechanics of correct grammar and logical sentence and paragraph construction are basic to good writing. In formal writing, the use of graphics, such as charts, tables, and photographs, can "spice up" prose and make it more accessible to the reader. Page layout and the appropriate use of "white space" can also aid the reader's eye and help make the writer's intent more clear.

Computers have significantly aided the paper flow within the organization and facilitated the revision of documents—a formerly arduous and staff-intensive effort. The addition of local area networks and electronic mail has greatly eased the written communication process and, though not exactly saving paper, has enabled staff members to communicate both with each other and with colleagues across the nation and around the globe.

Organizational communication is the glue that enables other dimensions of the directing component of management to proceed smoothly. When it works well, every other facet of management is enhanced; if it derails, other aspects of directing falter as well.

Directing and leading—coupled with leadership, motivation, and effective decision-making—chart the course by which the library moves from the tasks of today into the plans and dreams of tomorrow. The importance of good direction and leadership cannot be overstated. It could easily mean the difference between simple survival and a dynamic future for the public library.

For Discussion

- Theory X, Theory Y—which of these theories seems most realistic? Would a combination of theories be more to your liking? What effect, if any, does the situation have?
- What is leadership?
- What factors make you satisfied or dissatisfied with your job?

- What effect can participative decision-making have on employee motivation?
- How important are nonverbal cues to effective communication? Can you think of an occasion when verbal and nonverbal cues sent different messages?
- What are your two most difficult barriers to good listening? What behaviors can you adopt to improve your listening skills? What would you advise your coworkers to help them be better listeners? Your supervisor? Those you supervise?
- How can you improve your writing ability?

Scenario Six
Is Leadership Telling Others What to Do?

The Facts

The Zebra Public Library is located in a small midwestern city.

The Zebra Public Library has traditionally gathered the statistics that are required by the state on circulation, number of volumes, library hours, and so forth.

Staff have continually grumbled about this extra effort, seeing no particular purpose for it and perceiving it as bureaucratic "nonsense."

The library director has just returned from a leadership institute and is confident that the staff can be motivated to engage in a marketing audit.

Staff resistance to further "nonsense" is covert, but intense; the director is aware of staff feelings.

What Could/Would Happen If . . .

- The staff is directed that a marketing audit will take place and that they will participate.
- The staff is required to attend an explanatory workshop on the rationale for the marketing audit.
- The staff is requested to elect several representatives to a planning committee that will study the nature of the marketing audit and make recommendations as to the appropriate scale, given the library's fiscal and human resources.
- The director announces that the audit will take place and arbitrarily appoints a committee to do the work.

- The library board and community have representatives on the planning committee (to which staff members were elected).
- Representatives of another library that is involved in doing a marketing audit are invited to the Zebra library to discuss the problems and benefits of collecting the data.
- The director develops incentives to encourage staff interest and participation.
- The director contributes as much administrative support as possible to demonstrate commitment.

NOTES

1. Robert D. Stueart and Barbara B. Moran, *Library Management*, 3d ed. (Littleton, CO: Libraries Unlimited, 1987), 152.

2. Douglas McGregor, *The Human Side of Enterprise* (New York: McGraw-Hill, 1960), Chapters 3 and 4.

3. Malcolm S. Knowles, *The Modern Practice of Adult Education: From Pedagogy to Andragogy*, rev. ed. (Chicago: Association Press/Follett, 1980).

4. Charles A. Schriesheim, James M. Tolliver, and Orlando C. Behling, "Leadership Theory: Some Implications for Managers," in Rosie L. Albritton and Thomas W. Shaughnessy, *Developing Leadership Skills: A Source Book for Librarians* (Englewood, CO: Libraries Unlimited, 1990), 10-11.

5. William D. Hitt, *The Leader-Manager* (Columbus, OH: Battelle, 1988), 11-12.

6. Warren Bennis, "The 4 Competencies of Leadership," in Albritton and Shaughnessy, *Developing Leadership Skills*, 21-27. (Reprinted from *Training and Development Journal*, August 1984.)

7. Ibid., 27.

8. Dana C. Rooks, *Motivating Today's Library Staff: A Management Guide* (Phoenix: Oryx Press, 1988), 1-2.

9. Ibid., 2-4.

10. Abraham Maslow, *Motivation and Personality* (New York: Harper, 1954).

11. Frederick Herzberg, Bernard Mausner, and Barbara B. Snyderman, *The Motivation to Work*, 2d ed. (New York: John Wiley, 1959).

12. Peter Drucker, *The Effective Executive* (New York: Harper & Row, 1966), 143.

13. Herbert A. Simon, *The New Science of Management Decision*, 2d ed. (New York: Harper & Row, 1966), 39.

14. Victor H. Vroom, "Decision Making and the Leadership Process," in Beverly P. Lynch, ed., *Management Strategies for Libraries* (New York: Neal-Schuman, 1985), 506.

15. Stueart and Moran, *Library Management*, 48.

16. Catherine Sheldrick Ross and Patricia Dewdney, *Communicating Professionally: A How-to-Do-It Manual for Librarians* (New York: Neal-Schuman, 1989), 23.

17. Ibid., 24-30.

18. Ibid., 32-35.

19. Ibid., 36-59.

7 Managing Technology for the Client's Benefit

Information is becoming increasingly complex with the acceleration of change. This complexity is reflected in the totality of all information—good information, bad information, incomplete information, too much information, falsehoods, assumptions, and inferences—creating an environment in which the individual who has not developed the skills of critical analysis may find survival difficult.[1] All of this information is transmitted through some type of graphic record, which in turn is communicated through some form of technological delivery.

INFORMATION AND THE GRAPHIC RECORD

There are two basic elements in creating a graphic record: a recording surface and a means of altering that surface in terms of color, texture, thickness, or other characteristics in the process of making symbolic marks. At various times in history, such alterations have been made upon a number of different surfaces, including rock, clay, cloth, sand, paper, film, paintings, photographs, paper, television signal, computer disk, and so forth.[2]

In a very real sense, the graphic record moves between encoder and decoder, and its actual form is now increasingly diverse. Its permanence (even if limited) facilitates repetition and analysis. But some type of technological intervention to enable decoding is also required: appropriate wavelength light in order to read or appropriate machinery (hardware) that will interpret television or radio signals, project film on a screen, or run computer software. The simple communication model of sender→message→receiver that was originally formulated in terms of speech communication has become infinitely more complex. Allan D. Pratt, author of *The Information of the Image*, sees the expanded model as containing five elements:

1. The source (author, composer, painter, etc.)

2. The receiver (reader, auditor, viewer, etc.)

3. The medium (paper, magnetic tape, photographic film, etc.)

4. The language (English, French, musical notes, other symbol systems)

5. The message itself, composed of:
   - some language
   - impressed on some medium
   - with some purpose
   - intended to affect the image of some receiver[3]

If this more complex model is not sufficient, the dimension of receiver interpretation must be considered. In the more simple communication model, there is no guarantee that the receiver will interpret the message as the sender intended. but because the interaction occurs in real time there is an immediate opportunity to solicit feedback.

However, in Pratt's complex model, the receiver may be set apart in time and space from the sender through media intervention. Both sender and receiver have the latitude to manipulate both the medium and the message. Consequently, positioning the graphic record on the selected medium with consideration of the element of time can be fundamental to the communication process. Further, there may be ample time for the receiver to review and reinvent the purpose of the message—often with a dramatically different outcome.

The public library may serve as an intermediary in the communication process. It becomes an access point at which receivers interact with the various media that are receptacles for messages—and this access function increasingly involves using technology quite apart from technology's former role as medium. In the process, online public access catalogs (OPACs), CD-ROM databases, and online searching procedures are revolutionizing the interactions between senders and receivers. Library managers are moving beyond the role of responding to change and into the uncharted territory of creating change.

INFORMATION, TECHNOLOGY, AND ACCESS

The access function requires the application of librarians' expertise in connecting people with information—expertise that is so valuable in making sense of the surfeit of data that bombards each individual and organization. Logically, if information is power, then librarians should be in a very powerful position—a potential reality, but one that is not as yet appreciated by either the clients or the librarians themselves. This lack of recognition could be due, in part, to the relatively recent awareness of information and the latent power that it possesses.

Surprisingly, the idea of information did not excite the early writers about management. The classical works focus on the functions of management, including planning, controlling, coordinating, organizing, and leading—and information is not mentioned. Subsequent writers in the behavioral and human relations schools of thought recognized that management involved achieving results through people—in other words, communication. Yet the notion of information was still not developed. It is only in the later years of the twentieth century that attention has begun to focus on information itself.[4]

Change and the Need for Information

Decision-makers today face an ambiguity that was virtually unknown several decades ago. Turbulent change can be easily observed in the areas of technology, energy consumption, speed of travel, population, and agricultural production, to name a few. The greater the degree of uncertainty, the greater the need for information—and the more valuable the information that reduces the level of uncertainty. Rapid access to mountains of data does not address the problem; relevant information—meaningfully arranged data—is the basis of decision-making power.[5]

To more clearly explore this ambiguity, Tricker considers information at various levels:

Level One: *Basic data*—raw facts that describe events or states of being

Level Two: *Information as message*—the aggregation and analysis of basic data (examples: totals of monies, statistical summaries, reports). No thought is given to the needs of the recipient of the message.

Level Three: *Information in use*—linking the message to the receiver and specific attributes and needs of that receiver through the communication process; interpretation of the data.

Level Four: *Valuable information*—relating the information not only to the receiver but also to the organizational or environmental context of that user.[6]

As the awareness of information and its various levels gains in ascendancy, the mechanisms of information access change with the development of new technologies. However, these technologies have also promoted the evolution of information into formats external to the human mind. Once pen was set to paper, the graphic record superseded the need to retain large amounts of information within human memory.

The process of progressive externalization of information in which society is now engaged has implications for both institutional and personal development. Of the many thousands of "messages" that continually bombard the various senses, only a small fraction are actually perceived by the conscious mind. For those messages that do "get through," critical analysis is often overlooked.

By depending upon the external graphic record, we can postpone critical analysis—often indefinitely. This possibility does not mean that incoming messages are postponed; rather, images continue to enter conscious and subconscious levels of the mind at increasingly rapid rates. Although there is no compelling reason to analyze every message received—nor would it be possible to do so—the lack of critical awareness is a limiting factor. Moreover, the real constraints of data overload and finite amounts of time, when added to a cultural environment in which formal education has not routinely transmitted skills of analysis relative to the full spectrum of media, can make following a path of passive acceptance the most popular route. There is a growing need for a filter between data and clients' requirements.

THE PUBLIC LIBRARY AND TECHNOLOGY

Enter the public library. As an institution that has a history and tradition of collecting and creating access to the graphic record that has been available primarily in print form (from the papyrus roll to the book), the public library has only recently become an active partner in providing information in audio, visual, and electronic formats. Society has developed multiple means for storage and transmission of information and knowledge, so the library must develop strategies that will allow it to be proactive in meeting the future—a future that requires data interpretation as well as data storage. Consequently, the library administrator must now be engaged in managing technology as well as human, fiscal, and physical resources.

How can the public library become active in helping clients effectively make use of developing technologies? Ken Dowlin, in *The Electronic Library*, proposes six basic premises:

1. Individuals, families, and organizations will continue to acquire and use technology that can increase their ability to manage and communicate information. . . .

2. Information and access to information are crucial elements to societal progress. . . . The right to information by individuals must be established, codified, and understood by all in a democratic society.

3. Libraries and librarians have crucial roles in managing information and in providing access to information for individuals, families, communities, and organizations. . . .

4. Libraries and librarians will have to change their existing technology, and organizations, to remain relevant to society. An understanding of change and the processes that are involved in change is crucial for influencing change. . . .

5. The changes needed require a set of tools, and a toolbox to place them in context . . . [systems theory, hardware, and skills].

6. How these tools are used will be based on personal and professional values; their implementation will be based on strategies . . . that provide an organized implementation of the tools in order to lead to the promise of the electronic library.[7]

It is both a challenging and an exciting time to be a library manager. It is a time when old rules give way to new, when emerging technologies become routine, when expectations blossom and come to full flower—when the pace of change outstrips the ability to comfortably cope. The public library, if managers can learn to flow with the tides, can be a major player in the new century. The new public library will effectively utilize various storage and retrieval technologies in the effort to access and filter the wealth of available data. But the library also will have a responsibility to clients that goes far beyond basic storage and retrieval—a responsibility to assist them in becoming literate in the broadest sense.

FULL-SERVICE LITERACY

Traditional literacy, commonly defined as the ability to read print materials, is but one component in a comprehensive definition. In order to adequately address the complex issues connected with information in today's world, attention must be more appropriately directed toward a total view of literacy, a comprehensive picture that includes information presented in a full (and growing) range of audio, visual, print, and electronic formats—plus the cultural context in which that information resides.

Toffler's three waves of human development[8]—the "First Wave" agricultural society, the "Second Wave" industrial society, and the "Third Wave" information society—have all required, and produced, different cultural contexts and related messages. Indeed, Toffler's "First Wave" child needed to respond to a series of limited inputs and choices. The "Second Wave" child had a much wider range to deal with, but that overall spectrum was still psychologically manageable. However, today's "Third Wave" child is, as discussed earlier, continually bombarded by images and messages. In this message-rich culture, individuals have more need than ever before in human history for a repertoire of critical skills—literacy—that will enable rapid and automatic assessment of messages as they arrive.

Electronic Images

The transmission of electronic images—whether through air or via physical channels such as wire or fiber optics—has truly extended the reach of today's men and women, much as Marshall McLuhan declared more than two decades ago. McLuhan stated, "The personal and social consequences of any medium—that is, of any extension of ourselves—result from the new scale that is introduced into our affairs by each extension of ourselves, or by any new technology."[9]

In past centuries, the average person's reach did not extend beyond the immediate town of residence. This limitation has been (and still is) true for many library users; other clients have reached into nearby states or countries; still others have been dislocated by wars. Yet today the world has become the personal backyard of every owner of a television set. Society has moved from micro to macro scale in almost the blink of an eye. Satellite transmission has validated the theory of a global society—a new reality that has significantly outdistanced the practice of local and national politics.

Telecommunications devices deliver information and entertainment across vast distances. Electronically sophisticated machinery gives increased leisure on the one hand and seduces it away again through television and electronic gadgetry. It is no wonder that a print-dominant society, quite used to a relatively orderly existence predicated upon linear thinking and fewer choices, now shows signs of electronic paranoia as it is confronted by the fast-paced change and multiplicity of options accompanying the emergence of electronic images.[10]

Television has become the "paper target" because it is the most visible representation of electronic imagery. However, it is important to remember that a host of electronic hardware types—compact discs and other recording devices, radios, boom boxes, Walkmans, computers of diminishing size, video games, and a parade of other technological developments reaching on into the future—stand side by side with television in that electronic spotlight. In many ways, it is the spectacular appearance and effect of these devices that prove to be so intimidating; after all, print technology can be represented by pencil, pen, type, laser output, and so forth, but the effect is lower-key and seems to be less threatening. As an example, let us consider reading and watching television as competitors for personal time.

Reading mandates that the reader create a setting within the mind out of the pieces of personal experiences, memories, and fantasies. The text provides the skeleton; the reader must flesh out the story with internally generated settings, sights, and sounds. This is an active pursuit and is self-paced and nurturing of imagination.

Television, however, moves at a pace that has the potential to encourage passivity in the viewer. In addition, many television programs essentially train viewers to watch rather than to think or to do. Events unfold rapidly on the screen, allowing little time to assimilate the images, consider the message, and make a critical judgment—particularly if one's educational background has not developed these skills.

On balance, however, television must be perceived as a tool for communication, with strengths and limitations that are to be acknowledged and managed. Every medium has unique characteristics that can be utilized to best advantage, and the electronic media are no exception. The barriers of space and time have been shattered by spectacular developments in communications technologies. Satellite transmission, fiber optics, computers, and video recorders are but a few examples of technological (r)evolution. The behavior, thinking, and expectations of people have been and are being altered by proliferation of information and swiftness of distribution.[11]

Now that technological development has evolved—indeed, exploded—with increasing numbers and types of transmission and storage devices, the imperative to effectively employ these devices has also grown. The ability to communicate and analyze critically, both as sender and receiver, has historically been closely associated with power. This connection between literacy and power has multiple levels, the most apparent being the direct relationship between manipulation of communication methods and the resultant assumption of power. Beneath this surface, however, lies the relationship between message content and message expression. Still deeper resides the cultural consciousness that undergirds the message content. The public library has the opportunity to interact with clients on all of these levels and, indeed, needs to respond to the challenge to do so.

A society that develops a capacity for critical analysis of the quality in various communication messages is far better equipped to design its present and future than one that does not. To leave a charge of this importance to chance or simple evolution is a dangerous gamble. John Stewart Mill, in his essay "On Liberty," sets forth the premise that in a free society, where the flow of ideas is unchecked and the populace has access to them, the truth will eventually triumph because, in the end, men will be reasonable about ideas once they have had the opportunity to scrutinize them. History has not validated this premise, as nothing in human experience has demonstrated that wisdom, truth, rationality, or even common sense are necessarily linked to mechanical skills. Rather, it is the human mind, which has been taught to reason, to assess critically, and to discriminate between and among ideas, that leads society boldly on into an uncertain future.

THE LIBRARY'S RESPONSIBILITY TO ALTERNATIVE LEARNING STYLES

Although the medium itself and its range of effects must be given serious consideration, an important impact of any communication experience is necessarily tied to the message being transmitted. The message content can be approached from two directions: 1) Who decides on what is produced or published or collected? and 2) What is the substance of the content itself?

Librarians have been continuously aware that the process of selection is in itself a variant of censorship in the sense that making a choice necessarily precludes other possible choices. However, the total selection process begins in the authorship phase: what is written, filmed, recorded. Selection continues on into the publishing or production phase. The user enters into the process by selecting what is purchased, read, listened to, and/or viewed.

Taking this argument a step further, it is the mind of the librarian that makes the initial screening assessment:

- First, in the analysis of the library's collection—concerning what types and formats of materials are needed, and in comments to publishers/producers concerning making such materials available;

- Second, in the materials selection process, during which the decisions that are made necessarily eliminate other possible choices; and

- Third, in the filtering process that determines what data or materials will most closely meet the client's need.

It is then that the client enters into an assimilation phase (with or without critical analysis in place). Yet too often forgotten or otherwise given minimum consideration is the concept of learning style. Each individual has a preferred style of learning, one in which information is most effectively and easily assimilated. Some people learn best by reading, others learn by watching, listening, or touching. The overwhelming emphasis of public libraries on collecting print material has, in effect, disenfranchised those whose preferred learning styles are other than print-based.

In addition, the last decade has seen a growing awareness in the public schools concerning the identification of children with learning disabilities. These children, previously grouped with educably mentally handicapped (EMH) children, are generally of high intelligence. Their disability is a physical one, involving an inability to process printed symbols. Although there are many types of learning disabilities, most are related in some way to misinterpretation of symbols. When this type of disability is in force, access to information must occur through visual, aural, or tactile means. This entire target market has steered clear of the public library, rightly assuming that there is nothing useful to be gained. Yet the magnitude of this market is only now beginning to become apparent, and it has as genuine a claim on public library service as any other group. In fact, once formal schooling has been completed, the library may well be the only source of education and information that is available—a formidable challenge to those libraries seeking to reach out to the unserved.

Therefore, when the focus is on the client (as has been emphasized over and over), the consideration of learning style must be given adequate weight in selection decisions. Management information concerning client preferences should be one of the results of the marketing audit. Questions relating to learning disabilities may be awkward; phrasing that seeks responses about learning style simply indicates interest in the client. The library's responsibility to ascertain what preferences exist and then respond to those preferences with appropriate purchasing seems quite clear. This approach has not been the norm; it must be an imperative in the client-centered library.

APPROPRIATE TECHNOLOGIES

There is another parameter to be considered when weighing choices concerning both software and hardware: appropriate technologies. The notion of "appropriate" simply means that decisions are informed by the marketing audit, thereby taking into consideration identified client needs and what internal and external resources are available. De Gennaro stresses, "We have to keep all these 'revolutions' in perspective. The reality is that librarians cannot implement revolutionary changes in libraries. We have to introduce technological change in a way and at a pace that is acceptable to the communities we serve."[12] In other words, management of technology must work in tandem with what will best serve the client.

The fact that a technology exists does not make it an automatic purchase, either for purposes of better access to materials or in terms of formats. The data gathered through the marketing audit should be a virtual treasure trove when such decisions are being pondered. Looking at both access and formats, a number of issues need to be considered.

Access to Materials

If the library is presently operating with manual systems, would automated systems be appropriate? If so, what type and scale would best address the library's needs (keeping service to the client as the primary consideration)? Which of the library's operations should be automated: the catalog, circulation, acquisitions, interlibrary loan, other? Should these be separate systems or a single integrated system? Which of the following automation options would be most appropriate: time-sharing or resource-sharing (in which the library pays a vendor or agency for computer use and access), turnkey systems (a complete system, installed on the library's premises by a vendor), independent hardware and software purchase (which may cause complex problems of maintenance and compatibility), or in-house development?

If an online public access catalog is to be developed, will clients be able to access it from remote locations? Will the database be housed on disks or CD-ROM? Does a statewide database exist? If so, will this library's records be part of that database?

If insufficient expertise is present on the staff, should a consultant be hired? What human resources are available to help with retrospective conversion of existing records? What are staff and client attitudes toward automation? If less than enthusiastic, how can these attitudes be softened? What kind of training will be necessary for both staff and clients? What would be the most effective transition from manual to automated systems?

Automation requires careful planning and, as a part of the library's overall planning process, should move within the context of that process. The concept of involving staff members and representatives of the library's client groups in the larger planning exercise has been emphasized; that same concept must be applied to specific projects such as automation so that a sense of ownership is established. Further, it is the staff and clients who will work most closely with the system, so their preferences and attitudes must be seriously factored into the decision-making.

Ultimately, satisfaction with the system selected will be directly related to how thoroughly the library conducts the planning process. Good planning may be time-consuming and frequently will be costly, but it is the basis for careful and meaningful evaluation—and definitely worth the investment.[13]

Formats to Be Included in the Collection

Based on the marketing audit, what are the learning styles and preferences of the library's present and potential clients? What types and formats of equipment (e.g., VCRs: VHS or Beta format) do community members own—or plan to purchase in the next few years? Is one format increasing in popularity while another is declining? Have local schools been consulted to identify individuals with learning disabilities who would require audio and/or visual formats for learning? Does the percentage (in the total collection) of materials in each format represent the needs and desires of the community? Do community members know what is possible to expect from the library in terms of both formats and services? Is the library moving responsibly into the future by providing information on appropriate formats, without becoming embedded in tradition and outdated perceptions?

There will always be additional issues that are of importance in the local setting. What must be remembered is that decisions governing the purchase and implementation of various technologies and formats should be grounded in what is learned from the marketing audit. Although there may be a strong urge to be "on the cutting edge," good service dictates that both internal and external environmental data must inform those decisions.

The Myth of the Definitive Technology

The desire to provide the most up-to-date library possible is a worthy ideal; the reality may be quite different. As the discussion above indicates, the existence of a technology does not constitute an automatic decision to purchase it. At the other extreme, however, is the library manager who continually puts off making decisions in this arena while waiting for the "definitive technology"—why should the library develop a collection of videocassettes until the format question of VHS versus Beta is completely settled? (And, of course, there is that rumor that another format in $\frac{1}{4}$ inch may be coming along.)

In the real world, the rapid rate of technological development makes the entire issue of "definitive technology" nothing more than an illusion. Almost as soon as a format emerges and becomes popular, scientists in laboratories are busily working on yet another project that will "revolutionize" the industry. It is likely that the library manager who chooses to wait for the dust to settle will find yet another dust storm looming on the horizon. It is far better to rely upon the marketing audit to provide data on what clients prefer in the present and near future and purchase whatever materials will support those preferences.

This chapter has examined technology, with a focus on the client's benefit and discussion concerning the graphic record, access, literacy, learning styles, appropriateness, and formats. Managing in an era of technological change is both challenging and exciting—with more than a little frustration on the side. Yet it is within this milieu that decisions will be made regarding what the library will offer to its clients. The next chapter will continue this focus on the client through consideration of product development and distribution in the context of a marketing approach to management.

For Discussion

- What is a graphic record? How has it changed over the centuries?
- How are/were each of these types of graphic records accessed?
- Consider one piece of information and track it through the four levels proposed by Tricker.
- Consider Dowlin's six premises, which were published in 1984. How relevant are they today? Would you change any of the premises? Delete or add premises?
- Explain literacy in the context of the full range of media formats.
- Contrast the experience of reading *Gone with the Wind* and viewing it on film/video. What are the various strengths and limitations? Which do you prefer? Which format would you prefer to use first?
- How can the public library provide information that addresses the several learning styles?
- What technologies are most appropriate for your public library?

Scenario Seven
Whither Technology?

The Facts
Brown Public Library is situated in a semirural area that was originally agricultural in nature but has passed through several decades of heavy industrialization and today is becoming a mecca for high-technology corporations.

The library administration, in an attempt to meet changing community needs, has embarked on a planning process.

The library itself is seeking to upgrade its circulation system and is considering the purchase of an integrated system that will handle circulation, interloan, and an online catalog.

What Could/Would Happen If . . .
- A planning committee composed of staff members, trustees, and local community leaders is established to conduct a marketing audit to determine both internal and external needs.
- Representatives of some of the high-tech corporations are included on the planning team.
- The planning committee consists only of members of the administration and staff.
- The marketing audit includes a community study that does—or does not—ask the question: "What equipment—both computer and/or audiovisual—do you own or plan to buy within the next two years?"
- The planning team assigns a special task force to investigate current technology and societal trends and options.
- A local futurist is invited to serve on the team.
- Public hearings are announced and held.
- One or more consultants are hired in specialty areas, such as automation, marketing, funding, and space planning.
- A foundation is established to receive private donations and bequests.

NOTES

1. Kenneth E. Dowlin, *The Electronic Library* (New York: Neal-Schuman, 1984), 13.

2. Allan D. Pratt, *The Information of the Image* (Norwood, NJ: Ablex Publishing, 1982), 16-17.

3. Ibid., 19.

4. R. I. Tricker, *Effective Information Management: Developing Information Systems Strategies* (New York: Van Nostrand Reinhold, 1982), 21.

5. Ibid., 28-29.

6. Ibid., 29-35.

7. Dowlin, *Electronic Library*, vii-ix.

8. Alvin Toffler, *The Third Wave* (New York: Bantam Books, 1980).

9. Marshall McLuhan, *Understanding Media: The Extensions of Man* (New York: McGraw-Hill, 1964), 23.

10. Darlene E. Weingand, *Connections: Literacy and Cultural Heritage* (Metuchen, NJ: Scarecrow Press, 1992).

11. Warren K. Agee, Phillip H. Ault, and Edwin Emery, *Introduction to Mass Communications*, silver anniversary ed. (New York: Harper & Row, 1985), 14.

12. Richard De Gennaro, *Libraries, Technology, and the Information Marketplace* (Boston: G. K. Hall, 1987), 4.

13. David C. Genaway, "Planning for an IOLS," in *Libraries in the Age of Automation: A Reader for the Professional Librarian* (White Plains, NY: Knowledge Industries Publications, 1986), 139, 153.

Marketing: Phase Two

The discussion of a marketing approach to management began in chapter 2, with a focus on the planning process and emphasis on the marketing audit. This chapter will continue that discussion by looking at the library's programs and services (products), costs (price), distribution (place), and communication (promotion)—from a management point of view. These are the "4 Ps" that were originally coined by Philip Kotler.[1] The sum of these factors, along with the process components of the marketing audit and evaluation, provides an interface with the elements of planning that enables the library manager to successfully oversee today's operations and tomorrow's opportunities.[2] In a very real sense, it is planning that charts direction but marketing that makes it all happen. The integration of the planning and marketing processes creates a framework that the library manager can use to structure the library's operations over both the short and the long term.

DEVELOPING PRODUCTS THAT MEET COMMUNITY NEEDS

Once the needs of the community have been identified through the community analysis portion of the marketing audit, it is time to take a careful look at the library's products. What are products? The concept of product has emerged from the profit sector—those items that are developed by a commercial enterprise and then offered for sale. Transplanting the term to the nonprofit sector, in which the public library operates, is admittedly questionable. However, there are similarities that make the conversion reasonable:

- In both sectors, there is intended interaction between producer and consumer.

- The word "product" is derived from "producer," and the library does produce a range of services.

- The desired interaction is grounded in an exchange of com-
modities. In the profit sector, the exchange involves items or
services that are offered for purchase; in the nonprofit sector,
the exchange involves items or services that are supported by
tax monies, contributions, or other support.

The Concepts of Product Mix, Line, and Item

The library's products can be arranged within the three-dimensional structure of product mix, product line, and product item—or
circles within circles. Figure 8.1 illustrates graphically how these
three concepts relate to each other. Examples of library products can
be arranged as follows:

Product Mix

Product Line #1: Collection
- *Product Items:* books, videos, periodicals, films,
phonodiscs, compact discs, cassettes, pamphlets,
art prints, etc.

Product Line #2: Services
- *Product Items:* circulation, interloan, home-
bound service, online searches, reference service

Product Line #3: Programs
- *Product Items:* story hours, film series, literacy
tutoring, income tax assistance, art shows

This arrangement puts the various library products into context:
individual product items collected into product lines that express
commonality of purpose, and product lines that form the overall
product mix offered by the library to the community.

Once the overall concept of product is accepted vis-à-vis library
operations, the relationship of specific products to what the library
offers becomes more than an analogy. The library provides a range of
products/services to its community, including the collection, refer-
ence/information service, hours during which there is access to the
collection and professional expertise, story hours and other programming, and so forth. Some of the library's products are traditional and
have been in existence for many years. Other products have been
developed more recently, such as online searching, microcomputers
for in-library use, and databases on CD-ROM, to name a few.

Fig. 8.1. Product Mix. Adapted from an illustration originally published in Darlene E. Weingand, *Marketing/Planning Library and Information Services* (Littleton, CO: Libraries Unlimited, 1987).

Expansion and Contraction

In this time of rapid change, it becomes increasingly important that library managers and staff continually assess the products currently being offered in the light of community needs, developing technologies, and societal shifts. Too often, the library's products remain the same, with additions during times when money is available, but there is no real analysis of product timeliness and effectiveness.

Further, it is true in nature that organisms are born, grow and mature, decline and pass on. The same must be true of products. There is a time for a product to emerge, to develop and enjoy a peak time; there will be an inevitable decline because of changing conditions; and, finally, there must come a time of phaseout. In libraries, this life cycle may be interrupted during the decline phase because of staff reluctance to part with traditional services, and products may hang on long past the point of real effectiveness.

Therefore, it is crucial that products be regularly evaluated during the annual planning cycle, and library staff need to become comfortable with the concept of the product life cycle. The following criteria may help the process of assessing both present products and ideas for potential products:

Information Agency Operations:
- Compatibility with agency efforts—really our business
- Continuity—would not require interruption of present activities
- Availability of general know-how
- Ability to meet client service requirements

Potential Market:
- Market size/volume
- Location
- Market share (present and potential)
- Diversity—needed by several target markets?
- Assured market growth
- Stability in declining budget years
- Foothold in a new field, area

Marketability:
- Estimated cost vs. competition
- Presence of qualified personnel
- Ease of promotability
- Suitability of existing distribution channels
- Originality of product
- Degree of competition (present and potential)
- Life expectancy of demand
- Client loyalty
- Absence of opposition from competition

Production:
- Feasibility of product
- Adequacy of technical capability
- Development cost
- Adequacy of production capability
- Materials availability

- Staff availability
- Facilities: equipment/space availability
- Service support availability
- Storage availability

Budget:
- Effective return on investment
- Capital availability
- Payback period[3]

Intellectual Freedom: A Special Responsibility

There is also an ethical dimension related to product decisions that must be part of the decision-making process. Particularly in a community in which a vocal majority espouses one side of a controversial issue, there may be a temptation to collect materials and provide services and programs that reflect this point of view—and include few, if any, products representing other sides of the issue. One might even rationalize that taking this approach is "responding to community needs."

However, libraries are not subject to the will and/or persuasions of the majority; indeed, they have a responsibility to present the spectrum of views surrounding various issues. The "Library Bill of Rights" and the "Statement of Ethics" of the American Library Association are more than simple documents—they are living and breathing expressions of important ethical concerns and First Amendment freedoms. Whereas individuals and groups routinely hold beliefs and attitudes that relate to specific points of view, the library has historically had the mission to carry information representing multiple perspectives.

This mission can be taken for granted, and its importance may be overshadowed by daily pressures and responsibilities. However, when product decisions are being made, attention should be paid to this ethical dimension so that the decisions reflect not only cost and demand considerations but philosophical and ethical concerns as well.

Once the evaluation of each present and potential product is completed, those products appearing to be the most appropriate to the library's goals and objectives must be reassessed in the light of the twin factors of cost and demand. Of course, this is not possible until the cost to produce each product is calculated—which leads directly into the discussion of cost.

IDENTIFYING THE COSTS FOR EACH PRODUCT

Philip Kotler's "price" designation is often confused with the notion of charging a fee for service. However, although fees may be part of the picture for some product items, for purposes of this discussion "price" must be considered a synonym for "cost"—the cost to produce each product item. As noted above, there is no way to fully assess a product without knowing the cost involved in producing and distributing that product.

The most obvious example of cost analysis is found in the profit sector: All cost factors are determined, a profit percentage is added, and a price for the goods or services is set based upon those calculations. In the nonprofit sector, an inverse approach must be applied: The budget bottom line is the known quantity, and all possible library products must compete for a share of those monies. In both sectors, the cost factors are similar; only the decision-making process is different.

The Process of Assigning Costs to Programs

How can these cost factors be identified? Every business—and the library must also be considered a business—has both direct and indirect costs. Direct costs are those items that can be attributed to specific products, whereas indirect costs cover factors that relate to the library's total operations. Examples of direct costs include:

- rental of space or equipment

- salaries of personnel hired to work only in conjunction with a particular product

- additional supplies purchased in support of that product

Conversely, indirect costs are those factors that are difficult to assign to individual products because they cross over several (or all) products and include such items as:

- the operation of buildings and equipment, such as rent, heat, light, maintenance, and depreciation

- supplies from existing stores normally kept in stock

- salaries of regular library personnel

- supplemental services, such as municipal purchasing, billing, printing, and so forth

Direct costs are readily apportioned to each of the library's products, because they represent cost elements that are incurred as each product is developed. Indirect costs require special attention. One formula that may be used in the attempt to allocate them is a calculation based on (regular) staff time. When the time each regular staff member spends on each product is calculated[4] and weighted according to staff salary, the sum of time spent by the entire staff on each product can be reformulated into a percentage. For each product, that percentage can be applied to each of the library's indirect costs and the resultant figures inserted into the program budget.

The Program Budget

The breakdown and arrangement of costs by program (or product) is known as a program budget (see fig. 8.2). Although in marketing terms such a budget might be more appropriately called a product budget, this is not the language commonly found in library literature, so the term "program budget" will be used here. There are good reasons to create a program budget, including:

- the ability to compare and contrast different products on a cost basis

- the ability to demonstrate to funding authorities and to the community exactly how the money will be spent

- the ability to illustrate what products might or would be reduced or eliminated if the funding were cut

- the ability to illustrate what products could be provided to the community if sufficient additional monies were to become available

Although it is more time-consuming to develop a program budget than a line item budget, the time is well spent. In fact, even when a municipality requires the presentation of a budget in line-item format, the sum of each category (such as personnel) in a program budget can quickly be worked into the line-item structure. Further, the effective library manager will present both types of budgets at the annual budget hearing, with the program budget serving as the basis for the presentation.

No business would present a product for sale without knowing what the costs were (how could a price possibly be calculated?), yet libraries have blissfully operated for many years without having this information. Yes, libraries have had budgets, but they have typically been of the line-item variety, and the costs for each product have not been known. This lack of knowledge has made decision-making regarding what products to offer, which ones to downsize, and which ones to eliminate virtually a subjective exercise.

There is a flip side to deciding which products to offer, even when information from the marketing audit and relative cost factors are known. This flip side is demand. A proposed product may be very cost-effective and may be well suited to meeting an identified need, yet the actual demand must be considered. It is well advised to offer a pilot or trial period for a new product in order to determine whether appropriate demand will be forthcoming.

It is not an easy matter to decide which products should be offered to the community. With the full spectrum of information available, however, the library manager can make informed and objective decisions—and make them in the context of the planning process. Without the necessary cost data, vital information would be lacking and subsequent decisions less well informed.

Program Budget[1]

	Reference	Videos	Story Hours
Personnel	$10,000	$ 5,000	$5,000
Supplies	500[2]	200[3]	400[4]
Materials	5,000[5]	10,000[6]	2,500[7]
Equipment	5,000[8]	3,000[9]	500[10]
Indirect Costs[11]	5,000	2,000	1,000
Total	$25,500	$20,200	$9,400

Total Budget: $55,100

[1] This information is extremely simplified, and the numeric values given are simply for purposes of illustration.
[2] Computer paper, computer disks, signage, etc.
[3] Signage, promotional flyers, etc.
[4] Craft materials, puppets, etc.
[5] Reference books, CD-ROM subscriptions, etc.
[6] Cost of purchasing videos
[7] Picture books purchased for use in story hours
[8] Computer, printer, CD-ROM
[9] Projection TV, headphones
[10] Puppet stage
[11] Heat, light, rent, janitorial, etc.

Fig. 8.2. is continued on page 140.

Line Item Budget

Personnel	$20,000[12]
Supplies	1,100[13]
Materials	17,500[14]
Equipment	8,500[15]
Indirect costs	8,000[16]
Total Budget	$55,100[17]

[12]The sum of all personnel costs
[13]The sum of all supplies expenses
[14]The sum of all materials expenses
[15]The cost of all equipment
[16]Heat, light, rent, janitorial, etc.
[17]Equal to the sum of totals of each program.

Fig. 8.2. Sample Budgets.

DETERMINING CHANNELS OF DISTRIBUTION

The third component of the "Ps" concerns how each product will connect with the target markets—the clients. Kotler refers to distribution as "place"—a term that is relatively straightforward when the product is secured through a single location. But the concept of place becomes more complex when there are multiple access points, including both physical sites and other alternative delivery systems. Therefore, it is necessary to examine place in the context of product distribution and channels of connection between product and clients. There are obvious costs connected to distribution and access, and specific judgments will need to be made regarding which channel(s) within a range of alternatives will be selected for each product.

The Key Is Access

If distribution is not framed within the concept of access, the thrust of purpose is missing, and subsequent decision-making might be unduly influenced by cost considerations and laissez-faire. However, when access is held out as the driving goal, objectives and actions can be developed to provide distribution channels that meet client needs in terms of both time and point-of-use convenience.

There are nine factors that are concerned with the flow of decision-making from initial product determinations through the entire life cycle of the product. With access as the decision frame, these nine factors need to be included in the ongoing discussion and evaluation process.[5]

Factor #1: Quality of Service. Distribution must be viewed as an integral part of each product, for a product that cannot be used is of very little value. Therefore, when the level of access is high, the product itself is enhanced. This interdependence of product and distribution can be observed in several use measures: the nature of the information output (level of accuracy, language, appropriateness, etc.), the format in which the product is available (audio, print, visual, person-to-person, program, etc.), the type of access (building, electronic, mail, etc.), and the speed with which the desired information can be obtained.

Factor #2: Time, Convenience, and Resource Allocation. The barrage of sensory images and daily demands that besiege every person during every day creates an environment in which time and convenience needs are almost tangible. Client perception of product excellence will be strongly influenced by the personal time that must be expended to secure needed information. This time element can be defined as follows:

- *The time expended by staff in the process of providing information.* A well-educated and -trained staff working with appropriate library resource materials and knowledgeable in the skills of referral can retrieve the needed information efficiently and with minimum expenditure of time.

- *The time expended in overcoming physical distance between client and service.* The most efficient staff and the most comprehensive collection of materials cannot be of service to the client until contact can be made. The traditional notion of the library solely as physical place becomes less and less workable in the light of increasing daily demands and decreasing personal time. In order to address these constraints, it is imperative that multiple access points be established. These access points can be satellite physical sites, electronic networks, telephone service, and mail/delivery services, to name a few.

- *The real time that service is available to the client.* The first two dimensions of time can be dealt with through the careful management of tangible resources; however, real time is defined in clock hours—specifically, the hours that the library's products are available to clients. Several questions should be considered: How many hours per day? Which hours? How do the present or recommended hours correlate with the hours available to clients? Are there ways to effectively use technology to overcome time limitations? Careful analysis of these questions, as informed by the knowledge gained from the marketing audit, can provide a real-time access profile that is both efficient and effective.

Factor #3: Priorities and Planning. When a framework of marketing is established to guide the planning process and the setting of priorities, the spotlight becomes focused on the client. Yet even under these auspicious circumstances, it is important that clients become stakeholders in the entire process. How can this goal be accomplished? By involving representatives from the various target market groups at every stage of the process. In this way, there is continual informing of the process by clients, and access considerations can be updated as client needs change.

Factor #4: Human Resource Intermediaries. Access can also be addressed through cooperative arrangements and ventures between the library and other agencies or organizations. Cooperation might come from a number of sources, including:

- Cable television operations (linking information agencies and individual homes and/or offices)
- Computer networks
- Shopping malls (establishing a satellite physical outlet)
- Postal/mail services (for delivering materials)
- Experts in needed areas (such as finance, law, fundraising, technology, etc.)
- Human service agencies
- Government agencies

This is only a partial list. These collaborations can expand the effectiveness of both participating agencies and decrease areas of duplication. In terms of accountability and political sagacity, cooperation is definitely to be valued in today's information age.

Factor #5: Number and Location of Outlets. The word "outlet" is used here in a general sense as a descriptor for buildings, bookmobiles, storefront locations, kiosks, or even computer work stations—in short, any physical facility that serves as the access point between the client and the needed information. Client convenience, as determined by the marketing audit, must be the guiding factor in determining the number and type of outlets. Consideration of service outlets should be done at regular intervals, in conjunction with planning process deliberations.

Factor #6: Technological Delivery and Formats. The principles presented in discussion of Factor #5 also apply to "outlets" that are based in technology. The rate of technological development is accelerating so rapidly that new possibilities for distribution are continually entering the marketplace. Today's world includes cable television, interactive video, computer networks, teleconferencing, broadcasting systems, satellite transmission, facsimile transmission, videotex, and many combinations and permutations of these technologies.

The existence of a technology does not assure that it is appropriate for implementation in a particular library; however, each technology deserves serious consideration and analysis as one of a number of delivery options. It is important to acknowledge that the same developments that contribute to today's rapid social and technological change may hold the key to coping with such change.

New information formats, too, are continually emerging in the arenas of audio, video, and optical technologies (such as CD-ROMs and videodisks), to name a few. These formats offer expanding possibilities for clients with special learning styles and needs. Different formats are also basic to the storage and retrieval of information. Both storage capability and speed of retrieval are significantly enhanced by technological development, and libraries will be forever influenced and altered by present and emerging technologies.

Factor #7: Innovation and Change. All these factors coexist within a milieu of change and the need for innovative responses. If access to information is to remain in step, the willingness to experiment with alternative ways of thinking, coping, and responding is a mandate for survival. The library manager who would remain part of the information mainstream must learn to be proactive in the distribution of information and to be personally receptive to new ideas. Innovation is generally considered to be a small tail on a normal bell-shaped curve; moving closer to this extreme is a challenge to be embraced in the dawning of a new century.

Factor #8: The Finite Life Cycle. This concept applies not only to products but to all aspects of the marketing mix, including cost, distribution, and promotion. All components have applications that are "born" in response to client needs; they have a peak period of effectiveness and decline, and they ultimately must give way to more appropriate applications. This natural ebb and flow necessarily picks up speed as change accelerates.

Factor #9: Positioning. There are two levels of positioning: identifying the market niche for the library within the broad range of information providers and developing distributed products that also have a unique market share among the many possible competitors for client attention. The underlying assumption is that the library and its products cannot and must not be expected to meet all possible human needs. Discovering the best placement for the library is both a responsibility and a challenge that no library manager can afford to ignore.

These nine factors are integral to distribution decision-making and should be carefully thought through in the effort to develop creative and flexible approaches to information service. Placing the library's products in the marketplace is a complex endeavor; however, when client needs govern both distribution design and implementation—with a generous sprinkling of creativity and risk-taking thrown in—the result makes the library strong and proactive in effectively dealing with tomorrow's world.

PROMOTING AND COMMUNICATING

"Marketing" is too frequently defined in language that actually means "promotion," the fourth "P." However, such an approach is much like the tail wagging the dog. Promotion actually refers to the set of activities set in motion once all other marketing and planning components (other than final evaluation) have been completed. The actual definition for "promotion" is "communication"—communicating to present and potential clients that the library has identified community needs and has developed both cost-effective products and methods of distribution that respond to those needs. In this communication scenario, promotion is closer to an educational strategy than to the sales approach so popular in the literature.

Communication as Baseline

There are basic components to the communication transaction that need to be recognized:

- The *sender* initiates the message and selects the form of transmission.

- *Encoding* translates the thought into some type of symbolic form (words, pictures, sounds, etc.).

- The *message* is the series of symbols being transmitted.

- *Media*, or *channels*, are the paths through which the message moves between sender and receiver.

- The *receiver* receives the message from the sender.

- *Decoding* by the receiver translates the symbols into meaningful understanding.

- The *response* includes the reactions that the receiver has after being exposed to the message.

- *Feedback* is that part of the receiver's response that is communicated back to the sender (and often must be deliberately designed into the overall process).

If this communication model is to be used effectively in promoting the library's products, the target market(s) or audience needs to be clearly identified so that appropriate message content, message style, and media can be selected. It is also essential that a feedback loop be built into the process so that the audience's response to the message can be ascertained.

Aspects of Promotion

There are various aspects of promotion that can be considered as the library manager prepares to select appropriate strategies for each individual product. One or several aspects in combination may be incorporated in a promotional effort. As with the other components of the marketing mix, the focus must be on the target client group(s) if the message is to reach those for whom it is intended. Promotional aspects include:

Public Relations (PR). This aspect covers the overall interaction between the library and its current and potential clients. Public relations influences perception, attitude, and opinion by transmitting information concerning the benefits of using the present and/or proposed products. Interpersonal contact is a primary ingredient of public relations, for even the most excellent series of product ideas cannot be implemented without human action and interaction. The quality of this interpersonal contact influences in large part how well the client's needs and the product(s) offered correspond. The relationship between the library and its public is a cumulative one, with trust and mutual respect building over time. It is to be carefully cultivated and protected; in both good times and bad, it is the library's greatest asset.

Publicity. News coverage of the library's affairs secured at little or no cost is considered publicity. Included in the repertoire of possible publicity efforts are press releases, newsletters, columns in local newspapers, media interviews, bookmarks, posters, and displays. The range of possibilities is limited only by creativity and imagination.

Advertising. When publicity is paid for, it is generally considered to be advertising. Promotion in this form frequently needs to be more sophisticated and expensive than other types in order to compete with "slick" advertisements. It is possible to combine publicity and advertising by inserting a "bug"—a small, complementary note about some library activity placed within the body of a larger ad paid for by someone else. An example would be to mention within a full-page ad for the local grocery store chain that Thanksgiving food and decorating materials are available at the public library. Although advertising has not traditionally been a common mode of promotion for libraries, there certainly could be times when it would be the most appropriate vehicle. Furthermore, local media may wish to contribute the newspaper space or broadcast time as a public service.

Incentives. Another aspect of the promotional package can be effectively used in the market testing phase, when client attention needs to be drawn to a potential product. Examples might be: a new online searching service, with coupons distributed for free searches; an extended loan period for videocassettes; a free demonstration; and so forth.

Atmospherics. Critical to promotional efforts and integral to public relations, atmospherics include such elements as the ambience and environment of the distribution channels, whether physical sites or electronic connections. Atmospherics affect both attitude and perception and thus are essential to good client-product interaction.

Making It All Work

There are two organizational attributes that will make or break promotional efforts. The first, administrative supports, consists of both organizational commitment and the tangible backing of adequate funding and staff. Both elements must be present; having commitment without resources—or the reverse—necessarily results in a lopsided effort that limps along ineffectively.

The second attribute is the recognition that responsibility for the design and implementation of promotional strategies must rest with a single individual, even though a number of staff (paid and unpaid) may be involved with putting them into practice. This centralization of coordination is essential to an effective operation.

This continuing discussion of the marketing process has highlighted the "4 Ps" of the marketing mix: product, price, place, and promotion. Although integral to overall good management, marketing strategies cannot be successful without the monitoring and final analysis elements that are part of the controlling function of management. In the next chapter, these evaluation approaches are addressed in the context of accountability.

For Discussion

- What are the products produced by your local public library? Do they meet community needs? How do you know?
- Translate your list of products into product item, product line, and product mix.
- Take one product and run it through the list of criteria for assessing products. How viable and appropriate is it?
- Using the same product as a unit of analysis, determine what it costs to produce that product. Once this cost is known, evaluate cost/benefit in terms of demand.
- Does your library use a program budget? If yes, is every product represented? If not, calculate a program budget for the product selected above.
- Have any materials been challenged in your community in the past two years? Discuss the process and the outcome.
- How are your library's products distributed? At whose convenience—the staff's or the clients'?
- What channels are utilized to "tell the library's story"? Are the channels appropriate for the intended audience(s)?

Scenario Eight
Is Marketing More Than Promotion?

The Facts

Librarian Smith and Librarian Greene have recently become aware of marketing as an "in" strategy in public library circles.

Smith is director of a rural library serving a population of 1,900.

Greene is coordinator of public services in an urban library serving a community of 200,000.

Each has attended professional conference sessions on marketing; each has rushed back to the home library to try out what has been learned.

What Could/Would Happen If ...
- Greene hires a marketing specialist who will have as a primary duty the development of a media campaign.
- Smith requests board approval to divert 5 percent of the library budget to promotional efforts.
- Smith seeks LSCA (Library Services and Construction Act) funding for a pilot project to explore cooperation with the local cable TV facility.
- Greene restructures the organizational chart to closely match that of a library cited at the conference as having a successful marketing set-up.
- Greene writes an article for the local newspaper about the promotional campaign before it has been evaluated.
- Smith conducts a community analysis, using volunteer help; Greene hires a researcher to do a marketing audit.
- Greene holds a staff meeting to share what was learned at the conference and asks for volunteers to form a marketing management team to begin a marketing effort.
- In either situation: Several current programs identified as low yield by the audit are eliminated and other areas showing a favorable price/demand ratio are developed.

NOTES

1. Philip Kotler, *Marketing for Nonprofit Organizations* (Englewood Cliffs, NJ: Prentice-Hall, 1975).

2. The reader is directed to figure 2.1 on p. 15. This schematic illustrates the relationship between the elements of marketing and planning.

3. Adapted from Table 8.1, "Screening Form for Product Ideas," in Darlene E. Weingand, *Marketing/Planning Library and Information Services* (Littleton, CO: Libraries Unlimited, 1987), 67-68.

4. For a more detailed discussion on how to use a time log to identify the amount of time each staff member spends on each product, see pp. 77-78 in Weingand, *Marketing/Planning Library and Information Services.*

5. Weingand, *Marketing/Planning Library and Information Services,* 98-107.

A New Look at Control

The process of control, the specific focus of this chapter, has been necessarily present in every aspect of management that has been discussed. It is impossible to consider creating a mission, planning for change, working with staff, organizing operations, directing and leading, applying marketing principles and strategies, and implementing technology without also being aware of the controlling function. Because of this all-pervasive influence, deciding on a workable definition for "control" is not a simple matter. Therefore, a more global interpretation is preferred: Controlling is taking into account any action or process that alters results.[1]

In traditional orientations, control entailed internal hierarchical structures with strict lines of authority and reporting. In addition, the measures that were applied focused on inputs such as funding, collections, personnel, and so forth. With the shift toward a client orientation, different control measures needed to be established, and the elements of evaluation and accountability became primary considerations. By looking toward the external market, managers have liberated the control process from a stationary and generally rigid perspective and now have the flexibility to work in a fluid environment where innovation has an opportunity to flourish.

REALITY CHECK: OTHER CONTROL PLAYERS

The playing field does not solely consist, however, of the library manager, library staff, and clients. Other players who exert influence over library operations need to be acknowledged:

- Policy decisions are the responsibility of the library board.

- Funding availability flows through the municipal authority.

- Some monies are routed through the library system and/or state library agency.

- Federal legislation, such as LSCA (Library Services and Construction Act), is enacted by the U.S. Congress.

- Certification requirements (if any) for personnel are established by the state library agency.

- Local and state legislation is proposed and implemented by appropriate public authorities.

- Regulation of personnel practices may be affected by unions.

- Directions of library activities may be pressured by "unpaid staff," such as volunteers and members of the Friends of the Library.

- Even farther afield, education for library professionals is developed and provided by schools offering programs of library and information studies, and these programs are accredited by the American Library Association.

These corollary spheres of influence are real and may have a significant impact on the way the library operates. Therefore, any discussion of control must take into account the multiple threads that pull upon the director and, ultimately, upon the library itself.

Despite the various pressures and influences, however, the library manager holds the reins of control in terms of daily operations and long-range direction-setting. When working within the parameters of planning and marketing decisions, the manager can use control procedures in a creative way to assure the accomplishment of stated goals and objectives. Though in the past managers have relied on various sets of standards of control, the fluid nature of today's management structure focuses instead on the library's goals and objectives as the appropriate benchmarks. Indeed, the present rate of change has created a management milieu that is rather like permanent whitewater, with the manager using intelligence, experience, and skill to keep the library afloat.[2] This is as it should be, for each library is different, with different environments, different markets, and ultimately different plans for meeting client needs.

THE RISING IMPORTANCE OF ACCOUNTABILITY

"Accountability" is a term that has rapidly moved from the ranks of jargon into general usage. It is not restricted to public library management; the concept is routinely applied to the widest scope of governmental activity. Accountability is the acceptance of stewardship—the holding in trust and the effective operation of public holdings for the maximum public benefit. Accountability has become an increasingly visible and desirable value as fiscal austerity and shrinking budgets have diminished economic options.

The environment within which the library operates is important in the pursuit of accountability. This environment is one of the library's own making and includes intangibles that cannot be measured but that are necessary for quality performance. The basic foundation lies in those activities already discussed: establishment of the library's mission and roles; planning as a routine process; the development of policies; analysis of the community to be served; knowledge of the client; and implementation of marketing strategies. Establishment of this solid foundation of creative and sensitive library management provides a favorable environment in which to foster excellence. Excellence is certainly a superlative and may appear to be forever just beyond reach. Yet elements of excellence can be attained—once that prerequisite foundation has been laid.

As in Maslow's hierarchy of needs,[3] the several levels of performance quality build upon one another. If the basic foundation of library management has been well established and the necessary activities are no longer novelties that devour large blocks of staff time and energy to learn, understand, and put into practice, then actual and human psychic time is freed to devote to the pursuit of excellence.

There are many routes to excellence; for example:

- The welcoming smile and attitude of the staff member at the circulation or information desk (even though ill health or personal problems are marring the day).

- The concern and interest of the reference librarian in pursuing an elusive question to a satisfying conclusion (far beyond an average time limit or search of on-site resources).

- The willingness of the librarian(s) to serve on voluntary community committees and boards in order to both maintain a sense of local needs and influence community decision-making.

- The desire of staff to function as an integrated team, overlooking small real or imagined grievances or outbursts of ego in an effort to concentrate on the library's primary goal: meeting the needs of the client.

- The purposeful arrangement of library materials, furniture, and services to best accommodate client use (and not just staff convenience).

These are but a few examples; many others could be proposed. The common thread throughout is the willingness—even the urge—to go beyond ordinary expectations and to deliberately and enthusiastically seek out strategies to heighten user satisfaction and perception of library importance to the quality of life.

Elements of Excellence

When the foundation for excellence (as discussed above) has been laid and an awareness of possible routes to excellence has been fostered, then it is time to consider some of the elements that produce excellence: product effectiveness, efficient management, and avenues of cooperation. These elements, too, are part of the environment that will ultimately nurture the measurable aspects of library operations.

Product effectiveness includes the key components of accuracy, speed, completeness, availability, and integration:

Accuracy. The need for accuracy in response to inquiry cannot be stressed too strongly; accountability is poorly served by misinformation. Accuracy is a twofold responsibility: An inaccurate response to a request for information is inherently poor service, but there is an added dimension in that the client may not be aware of the inaccuracy and will accept the wrong data as truth. If a relationship of trust is to be established between librarian and client, there must be a basic assumption of information validity. The message of satisfaction that the library's client spreads to the community at large may well be the library's best method of promotion.

Accuracy is directly correlated to the librarian's professional expertise, but it is also related to the librarian's attitude and interest in checking and verification. Where the slightest doubt exists regarding the quality of the information, verification must be an automatic component of the reference process.

Speed. Why should speed be included as an effectiveness key? Today's world turns ever faster on the axis of change, and society has become increasingly dependent on the conservation of time. Consequently, people have less and less patience for spending time in the pursuit of activities that seem marginally productive and tend to want their needs satisfied yesterday. Therefore, a library that can provide an accurate product that can be delivered rapidly and with a minimum disruption of the client's schedule will be regarded as having a legitimate claim on public resources.

Completeness. In addition to accuracy and speed, the completeness of responses to inquiries can be a crucial factor in the provision of effective service. Partial information can, in some instances, be more detrimental than no information. The completeness of a reference response or a list of resources impinges both on the client's satisfaction and on product effectiveness. Every effort needs to be made to assure accuracy, speed, and completeness.

Availability. Availability means more than that the library's product is in existence and can be procured. It also refers to the convenience component, the ease with which the product can be obtained. To presuppose that clients will continue to travel to defined locations earmarked as libraries is to deny the premium on time prevalent in today's culture. Convenience becomes increasingly significant. The relaxed pace of earlier years has evolved into a frenetic, time-conscious one, and free moments are guarded and allocated with great care. The public library that recognizes changing societal conditions—and designs access to materials and services so as to accommodate these changes—will have a much greater probability of being acknowledged as an essential service in the life of the community.

Integration. If these keys to effectiveness are implemented into the library's mission and philosophy of service—and carried through the planning process—two forms of integration can occur: the integration of library activities into a unified approach that addresses the realities of client needs, and the integration of the public library as a vital resource into both the community structure and the fabric of individual lives.

Efficient management, the second element of excellence, has aspects beyond the acknowledged ones of planning, directing, staffing, coordinating, and controlling. Good management techniques can be practiced within the context of internal policies and procedures—and should be if the actual running of the organization is to be smooth.

But beyond competent management techniques lies the larger concept of expanding library scope and effectiveness through interaction with other levels and types of public and private structures. In times of economic constraint, the pseudoluxuries of duplication, overlap, and competition cannot be indulged or even tolerated. This message comes through from the taxpaying public and—even more directly—from the funding authorities.

Avenues of cooperation are the third element of excellence. There are basically two designs of cooperative activity that can be employed to reduce duplication and foster more efficient library management: interlibrary cooperation and interagency cooperation.

Interlibrary cooperation is established practice, not a new phenomenon. From informal arrangements for interlibrary loan to the establishment of formal systems and networks, an appreciation of local limitations and the potential benefits of cooperative activity has been growing in the profession for many years. Although it is true that problems of turf protection and political advantage have often deterred efforts toward formal cooperation, the recognition of the interdependence of libraries as the quantity of world information expands has been a continual stimulus.

Many public libraries are members of library systems, either single-type public library systems or multitype systems that mobilize resources to meet the needs of clients. This is not surprising, since adequacy of service is difficult to maintain even for libraries with a large or wealthy tax base. The many public libraries in small towns and rural areas cannot hope to provide for the total needs of their communities without tapping the opportunities available through system membership. Library systems, whether single-type or multitype, offer a menu of services. Possible items on this menu include:

- Sharing of resources (both materials and personnel)
- Supplementary collections
- Continuing education
- Centralized technical services
- Consultant service
- Service to special client groups
- Allocation of state and/or federal monies
- Administrative and support services

This list speaks for itself; there is a treasure chest of support available to supplement the services offered by individual libraries.

Interagency cooperation is less widely discussed in the literature but has a powerful potential for increasing organizational effectiveness. Discussed in more detail in chapter 4, this aspect of cooperation needs to be emphasized one more time because of its importance to efficiency of management.

In summary, accountability has been perceived by some as a threat of sorts, but it represents an opportunity to streamline operations, open new avenues of service and cooperation, and generally accept the stewardship role of the public agency. The public library can be a leader among the various municipal departments; it is a natural progression for an agency that already considers its clients to be paramount.

MEASUREMENT AND CONTROL

One of the tools available to the library manager is measurement—the process by which library activity can be accurately monitored and the results fed into an ongoing reporting system, which in turn becomes the bedrock for genuine accountability. As with many processes, measurement can be viewed as a continuum ranging from the very basic to the highly complex. Determining which points on the continuum are appropriate is a crucial local decision for each library.

It is when an inappropriate point is selected that measurement becomes a heavy burden to be feared and avoided.

Above all, measurement is much more than the simple gathering of miscellaneous data and the subsequent reporting of that data to official agencies. It includes the interpretation of that data in order to provide a cogent reflection of library activity. The concept of interpretation is an important one. The simple collection of statistical data is not measurement; it is analogous to the act of shopping for food but never cooking or eating it. As an example, some libraries collect circulation statistics and report them to other agencies without any effort at interpretation.

Although data collection is obviously an important element in the process of measurement, it is the interpretation of results that offers insights into the meaning behind the numbers. Interpretation is the act of translating numerical data into concepts that may be injected into the planning process. Simple data cannot in and of themselves ascertain either dimension or capacity regarding library operations, but through the interpretation process patterns and relationships emerge that can add to such comprehension.

Further, if the correlation between data collection and use is not identified and defined, major errors can be made in deciding what data should be collected; the decision of what to collect usually errs on the side of too much rather than too little. It is also not uncommon for useful data simply not to be collected at all. Such errors tend to add to the staff's perception of burden, and a negative cycle is established whereby measurement is avoided when possible, tolerated when not, but never viewed as a positive force for validation of effort or as an agent for change.

Measurement and Change

The reality of rapid change has been stressed throughout this book. Change is no less real in its effect on the process of measurement. The impermanence of estimating in an environment of change increases the value of measurement, and the monitoring function can be of vital importance to the library's short- and long-range growth. For example, if data analysis reveals that holdings are rapidly outstripping physical space capacity; that local demographics and business projections forecast a spurt in the 55-70 age group; or that community ownership of microcomputers and videocassette recorders is booming and the library contains primarily print materials—then various conclusions can be drawn that should have a significant impact on future library operations.

Further, routine introduction of data into the planning process can help managers keep a finger on the pulse of change and inform the design of proposed alterations in library products and delivery systems. If, indeed, we admit that change is ever present, there is an implicit mandate to effectively use measurement to support efforts to update operations and move forward. To do otherwise is to look backward through a darkened glass and to ignore those manipulations of staff, materials, and services that could cope with change and adequately serve a fluid society.

The Benefits of Measurement

The earlier chapters on marketing stressed the concept of benefit and its importance to full participation in the marketing endeavor. Such a perspective must also be communicated in the pursuit of measurement if data collection is not to be perceived as a burden. Given the importance of using measurement to creatively interact with change, and given the goal of intersecting the measurement continuum at an appropriate spot, taking measurements can assist managers in observing, documenting, and marketing the library to its world.

For example, suppose the director of Library A is seeking a funding increase from the city council and proclaims in the budget presentation, "Library A is a good-sized library for a town of this population and is heavily used; therefore, we need additional funds for more staff and space." There is little persuasiveness to be found in these generalities. However, the argument would be more compelling if rephrased this way: "Based on data relating libraries in towns of similar size and demographics, our library's collection of eight materials per capita and our ten circulations per capita annually indicate a high use rate. But neither the square footage of our building nor our FTE staffing is adequate compared to other libraries of similar size and service areas." These quantitative measures paint a graphic picture of achievements and inadequacies and, particularly if supported by charts and other illustrative methods of presentation, effectively demonstrate where funding is needed for excellence to become or continue to be a municipal goal.

In another example, Library B is being faced with a citywide budget cut of 10 percent. In the budget presentation, the director provides the information that materials circulation is ten items per capita and that the average cost of an item is $25. These figures set a value of $250 for each community member. If the director then shows that the present tax impact per person is only $15, this demonstration of benefit received provides a convincing argument that may not only forestall a budget cut but may well encourage a budget increase.

The ability to communicate clearly and forcefully to funders and citizens the accomplishments and needs of library service is a fundamental managerial asset. Such documentation is especially important in terms of marketing the library to its constituents. Perceptions of duplication and overlap of services can quickly lead to loss of support; perceptions of library purpose or mission as focusing on children and recreational readers can be damaging to the goal of marketing the library as an essential service. Measurement of library input and output activities can provide the evidence to erase misconceptions and to add weight to those aspects of service that present a more powerful image.

There is also an added benefit, one that is directed internally but has an ultimate positive impact on products and clients. Although it is important to assess the library's vital signs and current state of health, it is equally important to keep staff up to date on the effectiveness and efficiency of the library's services—with an eye to keeping the organization on track in reaching its goals and objectives. Further, if the entire staff (both paid and unpaid) is involved in the decision-making process as well as on the data-gathering end, then the channels of communication are open and those affected by the decisions can provide input all along the way.

Output Measures

Measurement in and of itself is neutral and cannot indicate "goodness" or "badness." It describes "what is" through the collection, analysis, and organization of objective, quantitative data. Value is determined by using these data for several tasks:

- Assessing current levels of performance

- Diagnosing problem areas

- Comparing past, current, and desired levels of performance

- Monitoring progress toward the library's mission, goals, and objectives[4]

For the library manager, value can be effectively addressed through a variation of measurement unique to the library field that focuses not on the inputs of budget, personnel, space, and equipment but rather on the outputs that are returned to the community. Such a focus emphasizes benefits—one of the keystones of marketing. These outputs, and their measures, include:

by
The extent to which the library is used by its community, as measured

- annual library visits per capita.
- registration as a percentage of population.

Materials use, as measured by
- circulation per capita.
- in-library materials use per capita.
- turnover rate.

Materials access, as measured by
- title fill rate.
- subject and author fill rate.
- browsers' fill rate.
- document delivery.

Reference services, as measured by
- reference transactions per capita.
- reference completion rate.

Programming, as measured by
- program attendance per capita.[5]

Once the manager has identified the questions that require data in order to be answered and has summarized what is already known, then informed choices can be made as to which of the measures will best address the four performance areas listed above—in the context of the library's own planning process.

The choice of measures to be applied also needs to be influenced by the concept of "level of effort."[6] The second edition of *Output Measures* goes into considerable detail to offer guidelines regarding various levels of effort that are possible. The manager should assess the human, fiscal, and physical resources that are available and enter into the level that is appropriate to the library's resources. Using sampling techniques helps to hold the line on expended effort, but each manager must face the level-of-effort decision in the light of what is realistically possible. The ultimate goal is to evaluate the effectiveness of library service.

EVALUATION

Evaluation is an integral component of the planning process; it is also both a complement to, and an outcome of, measurement. Both formative (monitoring) and summative (final assessment) evaluation are required if planning is to be an effective and meaningful management function. Quantitative measurement provides the planning team with the hard data needed to judge how closely the realities of library operation match the planning schematic.

The collection of appropriate data to use in the evaluation cycle may be initially perplexing. However, as with all collection decisions, the time spent at the front end of the process—during which assessment is made of what information is actually needed for adequate evaluation to take place ("adequate" being relative to the situation)—saves frustration and wasted energy farther into the process. Appropriate data collection should always be correlated to the desired outcome and must be linked directly to the question: "What do we need/want to know to make informed and intelligent decisions?"

There is nothing in the concept or practice of measurement that should cause prolonged uneasiness among library administrators or staff members. As with the planning process, staff involvement and ownership in the effort is essential. Prior understanding of the need, importance, and projected use of the data collection exercise is necessary. Continued communication regarding procedures and results smooths the way for long-term understanding and willingness to participate.

In this era of accountability, tied as it is to shrinking dollars and expanding needs, the requirement of hard data substantiation is becoming an absolute mandate. Evidence presented in quantitative rather than qualitative terms makes comparisons possible—between various libraries of comparable size and activity and between present and past performance. The issue for library managers and staff no longer is whether or not to become involved in measurement and evaluation but rather to what end and to what degree. It is the manager's responsibility to place all management functions and tools in the proper perspective and to use them wisely and well. There is little margin within the complexities of a changing world for the luxury of experimentation without carefully reasoned rationale. Human resources need to be conserved and nourished, with energies expended in directions offering the greatest potential for positive results. The craving for data to document the status and excellence of library service is very real. Accountability demands it and survival depends on it; the pursuit of centrality in community life cannot exist without it.

But there are elements of danger inherent in measurement and evaluation. The danger is in the outcome—what does interpretation of the data demonstrate? The results may or may not be to the library staff's liking; the possibility of proven inefficiency and ineffectiveness certainly exists. This possibility only makes measurement more important, allowing detected inadequacies to be rapidly corrected. Further, the data may indicate that certain actions need to be taken that may not be popular with some staff—such as requiring expanded or weekend hours, changing lunch hours, and so forth. But it is essential that such adjustments do take place so the library can maintain credibility with the community.

There is intense competition for every tax dollar, a fact that is increasingly acknowledged. What is less frequently acknowledged is the competition for the public mind, which involves attitudinal concerns, user and nonuser perceptions, and the bottom line, in accounting terms—actual quantitative and qualitative level of use by the community. Without the injection of measurement and evaluation into the planning process, the library's successful participation in this competition cannot be documented, and appropriate rewards of community support and funding may not be forthcoming.

The ultimate danger is much more than the outcome of the measurement process. It is that, without direction, the library craft may founder in the perpetual whitewater. If the challenge of navigating is seized, the manager's increased awareness and competence will make the adventure a challenge to be savored.

THE OPPORTUNITIES IN THE BUDGETING PROCESS

Budgeting is one of the most important games in the management repertoire. It comes complete with players, roles, strategies, and prizes. It is a statement of what the library is going to do for the next year—with price tags attached.[7] Budgeting is fundamentally the manipulation of revenues and expenditures for the maximum benefit of the library. The budgetary process normally results in incremental changes; however, there are budget years when a bond issue, tax increase, or income shortfall may cause significant adjustment to the revenue stream. If the budget can be thought of as a beamed scale, ideally kept in balance, the counterpoint to revenue ups and downs must necessarily lie with the control of expenditures.

In many ways, it is probably more accurate to think in terms of financial management rather than simple budgeting, as managerial skills are critical to the overall process. Financial management is concerned with a broad spectrum of issues, including:

- Accounting, auditing, and financial reporting

- Budget execution and control

- Cash management, involving the handling of cash receipts, investments, relations with financial institutions, cash flow, and general treasury management

- Risk management and insurance

- Revenue and expenditure forecasting

- Capital improvement planning and debt management

- Appraising the financial condition of a governmental jurisdiction

- Determining the actuarial soundness of financial schemes, such as pension systems

- Purchasing and procurement[8]

All of these issues have an impact upon budgeting and represent a level of responsibility that far exceeds the balancing of revenues and expenses. Although it is not the intent of this text to focus on the details of financial management, it is nonetheless necessary to emphasize the importance of these complex components to the overall function of control. In many library situations, either the library or the municipality (or both) will have fiscal officers with expertise in these technical areas. It is the manager's role to be sufficiently knowledgeable in order to engage in informed discussion with expert personnel. (This is true in a variety of situations; few library managers have the depth of automation expertise that would allow them to create the programming necessary to the various library functions, yet they must have sufficient understanding in order to interact effectively with computer personnel.) Good management requires a sufficient level of competence in a variety of subject areas in order to provide appropriate vision and direction—and the ability to recruit and hire talented employees with relevant areas of expertise.

REPORTING: ACCOUNTABILITY AND PROMOTION

Reporting involves more than preparing reports. It has deep roots in both accountability to the community and promotion of the library as a civic resource. Reporting has been defined as "keeping those to whom the executive is responsible informed through records, research, and inspection."[9] It is therefore an important aspect of control and uses the techniques of control to gather the information that will make up the substance of the reports. The development of such information for those records necessarily involves both research and inspection—through the already discussed methods of measurement and evaluation.

Therefore, rather than providing a catalog of specific elements of data to be reported, this discussion will more appropriately be concerned with the philosophy of reporting and the benefits to be derived.

Links with Accountability

Earlier in this chapter, the section titled "The Rising Importance of Accountability" stressed the concept of excellence in terms of product effectiveness, efficient management, and avenues of cooperation. Sound fiscal management is implicit in efficiency as well as in the sharing of resources through cooperative ventures. This stewardship of public monies is generally assumed to be the major thrust of accountability. However, although there is no denying the value of fiscal responsibility, the depth of accountability allows for a much more extensive interpretation.

Beyond stewardship, therefore, lie the deeper elements of product excellence, which in turn reflect the fundamental premise of responding effectively to identified community/client needs. True accountability involves a comprehensive analysis of these needs and the corresponding design of products that will meet those needs. Without this deeper interaction between needs and product design, financial management becomes a shadow without substance. The perception of benefits by the library's clients, as grounded in this interaction between needs and product design, results in the desired exchange of mutual benefits required by effective marketing. This is definitely the ideal scenario; striving for this level of involvement constitutes accountability in the most positive sense.

But how does this expanded definition of accountability link up with the philosophy and techniques of reporting? From the identification of needs to the evaluation of products, measurement and evaluation tools are used to gather data and assess results. With an eye toward collecting only those data that inform decision-making and demonstrate effectiveness, the judicious exercise of control creates an environment in which reporting to constituent groups becomes a straightforward and manageable activity.

The Potential of Promotion

Too often, libraries collect only the information that is required by an external agency, such as the state library agency, rather than concentrating on data that will help managers make decisions. However, for purposes of this discussion, we will proceed under the assumption that adequate and appropriate data have been collected and analyzed. The window of opportunity now swings open for the creative library manager.

Reporting is a required managerial function on multiple levels: from department staff to supervisors, from middle management to upper management, from the library director to the library board, from the library itself to its multiple constituencies. In many ways, reporting is essential to maintaining an adequate (if not dynamic) communication flow. The opportunity aspect lies in both the act of reporting and the style selected for sending the message.

Perhaps the most common mode of transmitting reporting data is through the annual report. But what does such an annual report typically look like? Columns and columns of numbers. The challenge to the manager is to reformat the same basic report statistics into an intriguing and compelling design that will prompt the public to read, view, and/or listen to the information presented.

Remembering that promotion is communication, promoting the library's goals and effectiveness becomes a continuous communication challenge. Responses to this challenge can take a variety of avenues. Although these avenues, as discussed in chapter 8, can carry the library's message to the community in many different ways, the annual report has the potential to be a particularly effective communication channel. Staff creativity can spice up statistical data with humor, graphics, photographs, and human interest stories. What started out as a set of dry statistics becomes transformed into a clever promotional piece that highlights the library's accomplishments. Whether conceived as a bookmark, newspaper tabloid, balloon, slick booklet, or some other format, the client-directed annual report conveys not only the information itself but also the intent to focus on the client's interest. Therefore, alongside the explicit message there is an implicit message sent as well.

In summary, reporting does not need to be a dull and tiresome chore. Rather, the opportunity is present to recast the essential facts into an appealing promotional tool with high client interest.

Let us now return to the definition cited in the opening paragraph—controlling is taking into account any action or process that alters results. This chapter has examined the actions and processes of measurement, evaluation, and reporting. These actions, in order to fulfill the function of control, must alter results. Therefore, they are not to be undertaken as simple exercises, as no more than responses to external requirements, or as something that "should" be done. Instead, with the ultimate goal rooted in positive change, these strategies need to be made part of the planning and marketing enterprise, influencing the total process over time. When this influence occurs, the process is continually informed and the monitoring aspect of evaluation can flourish.

=========== ஒ ===========

For Discussion

- Who are the control players in your library environment and where does the power flow?
- When is budgeting more difficult? 1) In affluent times; or 2) In times of fiscal austerity?
- Why is measurement particularly important in a world of rapid change?
- What types of data are being collected in your library? What should be? How are the data used for decision-making?
- What output measures are appropriate to your library's operations?
- What is the appropriate level of knowledge that your director needs in order to effectively provide direction to technical personnel?
- What types and styles of reports would be most effective in reaching your library's clients?

Scenario Nine

Is Evaluation Just Collecting Statistics?

The Facts

The citizens of a moderately sized urban area have viewed their public library for many years as a nice building to have in town—with nice branches to accommodate the reading habits of the housewives and children of the community.

In the past year, several events have taken place that have caused severe community stress and income loss:

- The major industrial plant has decided to relocate to another state.
- The unemployment rate is edging toward 15 percent.
- School teachers have decided to strike for more money.
- Local taxes have been raised 10 percent, but library funding has not changed.

What Could/Would Happen If . . .

- The library continues "business as usual."
- The library introduces a community resource file of daily events, clubs, and organizations.
- The library establishes an advisory council made up of representatives of local human service providers and institutes a comprehensive information and referral (I&R) service, either with outside funding and only on a pilot basis; or as a top priority in total library service and operated out of the normal budget.
- The library develops a job-help center, with information on available employment, resume writing, test-taking, etc.
- The library seeks a referendum for expanded hours of operation (based on the provision of existing, not expanded, services).
- The library plans to seek an increased mill rate one year after the I&R service is established.
- The library begins to collect and report data based on output, rather than input, measures.
- The library develops a creative annual report to "tell the library's story."
- The library recasts its budget into program budget format, and an effective presentation is made at the annual budget hearing.

NOTES

1. Robert D. Stueart and Barbara B. Moran, *Library Management,* 3d ed. (Littleton, CO: Libraries Unlimited, 1987), 194.

2. Peter B. Vaill, *Managing as a Performing Art* (San Francisco: Jossey-Bass, 1991), 2.

3. Abraham H. Maslow, *Motivation and Personality,* 2d ed. (New York: Harper & Row, 1970), 35-58.

4. Nancy A. Van House et al., *Output Measures for Public Libraries: A Manual of Standardized Procedures,* 2d ed. (Chicago: American Library Association, 1987), 1.

5. Ibid., 3-4.

6. Ibid., 5-7.

7. Frederick S. Lane, ed., *Current Issues in Public Administration*, 4th ed. (New York: St. Martin's Press, 1990), 363.

8. Ibid., 364.

9. Luther Gulick and Lyndall Urwick, eds., *Papers on the Science of Administration* (New York: Institute of Public Administration, Columbia University Press, 1937), as cited in Robert D. Stueart and Barbara B. Moran, *Library Management*, p. 12.

The Public Library: An Essential Service

The title of this chapter asserts that the public library is an essential service—but what does "essential" mean? A dictionary definition includes the following phrases: "the intrinsic, fundamental nature of something . . . necessary to make a thing what it is . . . indispensable . . . requisite."[1] However, rather than being recognized as an essential service to the community, today's public library lies somewhere on a continuum between being peripheral and being important to community life. Although some public libraries may have attained a high level of influence locally, the numerous reports of cuts in library funding attest to the gaps that often exist in community support. If the public library is to become truly essential to its community, thereby becoming indispensable and intrinsic to the community's nature, there is much to be done.

In these chapters, elements of management have been discussed within the overall context of focusing on the client. Traditional managerial functions have been viewed through the twin lenses of the combined marketing and planning processes. These two fundamental changes in the approach to effective management signal a paradigm shift that goes beyond the simple tension between authoritative and participative administrative styles—a paradigm shift that holds great promise for establishing the public library as an essential service in its community.

PARADIGMS AND PUBLIC LIBRARIES

A paradigm is defined as "a pattern, example, or model." Historically, paradigms have had great influence by promoting replication on a broad scale. With sufficient replication, a new norm is established, thereby concluding a process of change from one paradigm to another.

How does this concept relate to public libraries? The public library has traditionally been viewed as a public good, in the same general sense as parenthood, the national flag, and apple pie. Citizens speak with pride of the local library, particularly with reference to the building itself, whether or not they have ever entered its door. Civic pride, however, has often been insufficient to sustain a positive vote when increased library funding is needed. This paradigm of "goodness" has certain abstract qualities, and although this abstraction lives successfully within idealism, it falters when faced with hard realism. Therefore, when the fiscal picture is tight, idealistic attitudes frequently fall victim to the need for hard choices.

Complementing and reinforcing this idealistic paradigm has been the library's conventional approach to both management and public service. Given the belief in the library as a public good, it has logically followed that citizens "should" use the library; all that is really necessary is to inform the public of what is available, the hours of operation, and so forth (the outdated view of marketing). The expectation has been that people would come to the library in order to receive its services once the "better mousetrap" had been built.

In terms of management style, library directors have tended to adopt standard hierarchical and authoritarian organizational patterns, and it has not been unusual that the convenience of staff has taken precedence over the convenience of users. Although some outreach efforts and programming have been part of this scenario, the overriding intent has been to bring customers into the library.

If the library is to overcome the sense of financial apathy that accompanies simple civic idealism, it is to the paradigm shift that attention must be directed. Library managers need to recognize and adopt the new paradigm as the guiding principle of proactive management. In this new paradigm, client needs are paramount, and marketing and planning principles guide decision-making. The library's products are designed to meet those client needs identified through a community study and analysis of the external and internal environments. Distribution systems are created to link clients and the library's products in the most effective and convenient (for the client) way. Costs for each product are calculated so that cost/benefit analyses can be constructed within the format of a program budget. Promotion of the library's services is handled as a communication process and occurs as the concluding phase of the marketing sequence.

The new paradigm also requires a different management style. Participation by all employees through management teams and alternative organizational structures, such as orbit or matrix, encourages everyone affected by decisions to engage in the development of those decisions. This shift to a flatter organizational chart has the result of distributing authority (as well as responsibility) across levels of staff. Communication flows in all directions—vertically, horizontally, and diagonally—enhancing staff contributions to decision-making and fostering a shared vision of the library's mission and goals.

In addition, when the library puts together a planning team that also incorporates community members, there is an opportunity for ongoing assessment of community needs and a broadening of decision-making.

THE NEW PARADIGM AND THE ESSENTIAL PUBLIC LIBRARY

The new paradigm clearly benefits the library and helps it move into a more central position in the community power structure—but what is the reciprocal benefit to the community itself?

The claim can be made that well over three-fourths of the world's people, in the face of accelerating change, are greatly deficient in the knowledge they require for their and society's future well-being. This accelerating change is triggered by (among other things):

- Accelerating global change and advances in the social, political, technological, governmental, economic, and environmental realms, as well as widening gaps between the information and economic rich and poor, rapid displacements, and progress.

- Moving away from a monocultural control system toward a multicultural one.

- The overlapping development of a multiplicity of new eras (information age, space age, computer age, bioage, etc.).[2]

This deficiency becomes increasingly serious as we move more and more deeply into these new eras, where both individual citizens and the municipality have an increasing need for accurate, extensive, and complete information. Where they will seek out this information will vary, from extremely informal sources (such as friends, relatives, and so forth) to the more formal information-dispensing agencies, of which the library is certainly one. If, however, the library has become the information core of its community and the point of first contact when an information need arises, then the securing of appropriate information is simplified for both citizens and municipal officials. This would definitely be a significant benefit.

In very real terms, this exchange of mutual benefits illustrates the value of the new paradigm of library service. With the shift to the new paradigm of interaction between the library and the community, several things happen:

- By identifying and responding to community needs, the library begins to demonstrate an exchange of mutual benefits (the foundation of true marketing).

- By focusing on the client, the library moves 180 degrees from the outdated approach to service, and products are designed and delivered to the client in the most effective manner.

- By promoting community awareness of benefits—and delivering those benefits—the library moves ever closer to the core of community life.

- Through routine evaluation of its services, the library assures a high level of excellence and guarantees quality.

To be essential is not easy; it requires commitment, dedication, and a deep desire to serve the community in a very personal and compelling way. It is a challenge for both this decade and the next century. Without this blending of library commitment and client perception of benefit, the library cannot attain the goal that it seeks: centrality in the community. Using the concepts and strategies discussed in the preceding chapters, the library manager has the tools to make the leap to the new paradigm—and it is this paradigm that will carry the library forward as essential to the community's quality of life in an information society.

For Discussion

- How does the emerging information society affect the community? the public library?
- What services in your community would be considered "essential" today?
- On the following scale of 1 to 10, where would you place your local public library?

  1____2____3____4____5____6____7____8____9____10
  Peripheral   Important   Essential
- What other societal paradigms are currently in the process of changing?
- How can a library operating under the new paradigm mount a successful bond issue?

Scenario Ten
It's Your Turn!

The Facts

You are a newly appointed library director in a community of your choice.

You have just finished reading this book and have lots of ideas.

You are about to implement an administrative climate and style that will include what you have learned regarding:

- Planning
- Client-focus
- Organizing
- Staffing
- Directing and leading
- Managing technology
- Marketing
- Controlling

You are determined to make your library an essential service in your community.

Describe what you will do to make this happen . . .

. . . and Good Luck!

NOTES

1. *Webster's New Twentieth Century Dictionary*, unabridged, 2d ed. (Cleveland, OH: Collins/World, 1975), 624.

2. Earl C. Joseph, "Some Major Trends, Issues & Change Forces: Education Futures," *Future Trends Newsletter*, 23:6 (June 1992), 1.

Suggestions for Further Reading

Chapter 1: Evolution of a Mission

Buckland, Michael K. *Library Services in Theory and Context*, 2d ed. (New York: Pergamon Press, 1988).

Greer, Roger, and Florence DeHart. *Information Systems: The Common Theory Base for Bibliographies, Libraries, Data Bases and Artificial Intelligence Based Systems* (Metuchen, NJ: Scarecrow Press, in press).

Pratt, Allan D. *The Information of the Image* (Norwood, NJ: Ablex Publishing, 1982).

Toffler, Alvin. *The Third Wave* (New York: Bantam Books, 1980).

Chapter 2: Planning for Change

Hendrickson, Kent, ed. *Creative Planning for Library Administration: Leadership for the Future* (New York: Haworth Press, 1990).

McClure, Charles R., et al. *Planning & Role Setting for Public Libraries* (Chicago: American Library Association, 1987).

Molz, Redmond Kathleen. *Library Planning and Policy Making: The Legacy of the Public and Private Sectors* (Metuchen, NJ: Scarecrow Press, 1990).

Musumeci, Jo Ann. "Environmental Scanning for Libraries: Steering Through Change and Uncertainty," *Minnesota Libraries* 28 (Winter 1987-1988), 376-384.

Sheldon, Brooke E. "Strategic Planning for Public Library Services in the 21st Century," *Journal of Library Administration* 11:1-2 (1989), 199-208.

Toffler, Alvin. *The Adaptive Corporation* (New York: Bantam Books, 1985).

Vaill, Peter B. *Managing as a Performing Art: New Ideas for a World of Chaotic Change* (San Francisco: Jossey-Bass, 1991).

Chapter 3: Focus on the Client

Gould, Roger. *Transformations: Growth and Change in Adult Life* (New York: Simon & Schuster, 1978).

Knowles, Malcolm S. *The Modern Practice of Adult Education: From Pedagogy to Andragogy*, rev. ed. (Chicago: Association Press/Follett, 1980).

Levinson, Daniel J., et al. *The Seasons of a Man's Life* (New York: Alfred A. Knopf, 1978).

Neugarten, Bernice, ed. *Middle Age and Aging* (Chicago: University of Chicago Press, 1966).

Sheehy, Gail. *Passages: Predictable Crises of Adult Life* (New York: E. P. Dutton, 1976).

Vaillant, George E. *Adaptation to Life: How the Best and the Brightest Came of Age* (Boston: Little, Brown, 1977).

Chapter 4: Organizing for Effective Operations

Block, Peter. *The Empowered Manager: Positive Political Skills at Work* (San Francisco: Jossey-Bass, 1987).

Cassell, Kay Ann, and Elizabeth Futas. *Developing Public Library Collections, Policies, and Procedures* (New York: Neal-Schuman, 1991).

Katz, Bill, ed. *The How-to-Do-It Manual for Small Libraries* (New York: Neal-Schuman, 1988).

Lane, Frederick S., ed. *Current Issues in Public Administration*, 3d ed. (New York: St. Martin's Press, 1986).

____. *Current Issues in Public Administration*, 4th ed. (New York: St. Martin's Press, 1990).

Chapter 5: Staffing for Service

Alvarez, Robert S. *Library Boss: Thoughts on Library Personnel* (San Francisco: Administrator's Digest Press, 1987)

Conroy, Barbara. *Learning Packaged to Go: A Directory and Guide to Staff Development and Training Packages* (Phoenix: Oryx Press, 1983).

Conroy, Barbara, and Barbara Schindler Jones. *Improving Communication in the Library* (Phoenix: Oryx Press, 1986).

LeBreton, Preston P. *The Assessment and Development of Professionals: Theory and Practice* (Seattle: University of Washington, 1976).

White, Herbert S. *Library Personnel Management* (White Plains, NY: Knowledge Industry Publications, 1985).

White, Herbert S., ed. *Education for Professional Librarians* (White Plains, NY: Knowledge Industry Publications, 1986).

Chapter 6: Directing and Leading

Albritton, Rosie L., and Thomas W. Shaughnessy. *Developing Leadership Skills: A Source Book for Librarians* (Englewood, CO: Libraries Unlimited, 1990).

Anderson, A. J. *Problems in Library Management* (Littleton, CO: Libraries Unlimited, 1981).

Blanchard, Kenneth, and Spencer Johnson. *The One Minute Manager* (New York: Berkley, 1982).

Lynch, Beverly P., ed. *Management Strategies for Libraries: A Basic Reader* (New York: Neal-Schuman, 1985).

Stueart, Robert D., and Barbara B. Moran. *Library Management*, 3d ed. (Littleton, CO: Libraries Unlimited, 1987).

____. *Library Management*, 4th ed. (Englewood, CO: Libraries Unlimited, 1993).

Chapter 7: Managing Technology for the Client's Benefit

De Gennaro, Richard. *Libraries, Technology, and the Information Marketplace: Selected Papers* (Boston: G. K. Hall, 1987).

Dowlin, Kenneth E. *The Electronic Library: The Promise and the Process* (New York: Neal-Schuman, 1984).

Dyer, Hilary, and Gwyneth Tseng. *New Horizons for the Information Profession: Meeting the Challenge of Change* (London: Taylor Graham, 1988).

Oboler, Eli M. *To Free the Mind: Libraries, Technology and Intellectual Freedom* (Littleton, CO: Libraries Unlimited, 1983).

Tricker, R. I. *Effective Information Management: Developing Information Systems Strategies* (New York: Van Nostrand Reinhold, 1982).

Weingand, Darlene E. *Connections: Literacy and Cultural Heritage* (Metuchen, NJ: Scarecrow Press, 1992).

Chapter 8: Marketing: Phase Two

Fox, Beth Wheeler. *The Dynamic Community Library* (Chicago: American Library Association, 1988).

Kotler, Philip. *Marketing for Nonprofit Organizations*, 2d ed. (Englewood Cliffs, NJ: Prentice-Hall, 1982).

___. *Marketing Management: Analysis, Planning, Implementation, and Control*, 6th ed. (Englewood Cliffs, NJ: Prentice-Hall, 1988).

Kotler, Philip, and Alan R. Andreasen. *Strategic Marketing for Nonprofit Organizations*, 3d ed. (Englewood Cliffs, NJ: Prentice-Hall, 1987).

Weingand, Darlene E. *Marketing/Planning Library and Information Services* (Littleton, CO: Libraries Unlimited, 1987).

Chapter 9: A New Look at Control

Christensen, John. "Use of Statistics by Librarians," *Journal of Library Administration* 9:2 (1988), 85-90.

Fingerman, Joel. "Painting the Picture—Personal Computers and Graphical Presentation of Statistics," *Library Administration and Management* 3 (Fall 1989), 199-204.

Glazier, Jack D., and Ronald R. Powell. *Qualitative Research in Information Management* (Englewood, CO: Libraries Unlimited, 1992).

Hamon, Peter, Darlene E. Weingand, and Al Zimmerman. *Budgeting and the Political Process in Libraries: Simulation Games* (Englewood, CO: Libraries Unlimited, 1992).

Line, Maurice B. *Library Surveys*, 2d ed. (London: Clive Bingley, 1982).

Rosenberg, Philip. *Cost Finding for Public Libraries: A Manager's Handbook* (Chicago: American Library Association, 1985).

Van House, Nancy A., et al. *Output Measures for Public Libraries*, 2d ed. (Chicago: American Library Association, 1987).

Chapter 10: The Public Library: An Essential Service

Hale, Martha L. "Broadening Support Among Community Stakeholders," in LAMA President's Papers for 1985, *Managing Community Coalitions* (Chicago: American Library Association, 1985).

___."Paradigmatic Shift in Library & Information Science," in C. R. McClure and P. Hernon, eds., *Library/Information Science Research: Perspectives and Strategies for Improvement* (Norwood, NJ: Ablex Publishing, 1991).

Trezza, Alphonse F., ed. *Issues for the New Decade: Today's Challenge, Tomorrow's Opportunity* (Boston: G. K. Hall, 1991).

Weingand, Darlene E. *Administration of the Small Public Library*, 3d ed. (Chicago: American Library Association, 1992).

Index